S0-CBJ-999

Living in
God's Graces

pil

Publications International, Ltd.

Contributing writers: Elaine Wright Colvin and Elaine Creasman

Photo credits
Sharon Broutzas: 28, 38, 39, 45, 54, 58, 63, 66, 67, 68, 80, 96, 98, 102, 107, 108, 109, 114, 115, 117, 119, 123, 124, 128, 131, 135, 142, 147, 150, 152, 154, 158, 163, 167, 168, 174, 178, 182, 183, 186, 187, 188, 190, 194, 196, 198, 201, 202, 210, 223, 230, 235, 236, 242, 250, 251, 267, 272, 274, 276, 287, 290, 309, 318, 319; **Ed Cooper:** 75, 118, 127, 130, 132, 136, 140, 143, 155, 159, 161, 172, 173, 257, 271, 277, 289; **ImageState:** Wayne Aldridge: 37; Robert Beckhard: 86 (top); Mitch Diamond: 193; Dick Dickinson: 27; Chad Ehlers: 76, 176, 203, 266, 285; Bob Firth: 26, 89, 307; Willie Holdman: 175; Hollenbeck Photography: 279; I.T.P.: 139; Miwako Ikeda: 184, 220; Bob Jacobson: 247; Greg Johnston: 245; Steve Lucas: 55; Zeva Oelbaum: 280; Ron Sanford: 85, 312; Johnny Stockshooter: 219; Paul Thompson: 134; Tom Till: 300; Valder/Tormey: 110, 288; Hilary Wilkes: 303; **SuperStock:** 16, 18, 19, 21, 23, 24, 31, 34, 43, 46, 47, 49, 53, 62, 69, 79, 82, 83, 87, 88, 90, 92, 93, 94, 97, 103, 104, 105, 111, 113, 125, 138, 144, 146, 162, 166, 169, 179, 185, 189, 191, 192, 197, 212, 225, 227, 228, 229, 237, 240, 244, 246, 249, 252, 256, 258, 261, 263, 265, 273, 281, 282, 301, 305, 310, 314, 315, 316, 317, 320; Christie's Images: 25, 221, 294; Musee d'Orsay, Paris/ET Archive, London: 22; National Gallery, London/Bridgeman Art Library, London: 286; Charles Neal: 208.

Additional photography by Sacco Production/Chicago; Brian Warling/Brian Warling Photography.

Copyright © 2004 Publications International, Ltd. All rights reserved. This book may not be reproduced or quoted in whole or in part by any means whatsoever without written permission from:

Louis Weber, CEO
Publications International, Ltd.
7373 North Cicero Avenue
Lincolnwood, Illinois 60712

Permission is never granted for commercial purposes.

Manufactured in China.

8 7 6 5 4 3 2 1

ISBN: 1-4127-1019-7

Library of Congress Control Number: 2004102741

Acknowledgments

Page 17: From *See You Later, Jeffrey* by Fran Caffey Sandin. Copyright © 1988 Tyndale House Publishers. Used by permission of the author.

Page 20: From *Teenagers Pray.* Copyright © 1955, 1964 Concordia Publishing House. Used by permission.

Page 28, 190: From *Give Happiness a Chance* by Phil Bosmans. Copyright © 1980. Used by permission of the author.

Pages 29, 191: From *Ruth Bell Graham's Collected Poems* by Ruth Graham Bell. Copyright © 1977, 1992, 1997, 1998 Baker, a division of Baker Book House Company. Used by permission.

Page 35: "Pass It On," lyrics by Kurt Kaiser. Copyright © 1969 Bud John Songs, Inc. Used by permission. All rights reserved.

Pages 54, 87: From *My Utmost for His Highest* by Oswald Chambers, edited by James Reimann. Copyright 1992 Oswald Chambers Publications Assn., Ltd. Original edition copyright © 1935 Dodd Mead & Co., renewed © 1963 Oswald Chambers Publications Assn., Ltd. Used by permission of Discovery House Publishers, Grand Rapids, MI. All rights reserved.

Page 62: From *She Wanted to Read* by Ella Kaiser Carruth. Copyright © 1966 Abingdon Press. Used by permission.

Pages 70–71, 176: From *The Living Faith* by Lloyd C. Douglas. Copyright © 1955, renewed 1983 by Betty Douglas Wilson and Virginia Douglas Dawson. Used by permission of Houghton Mifflin Company. All rights reserved.

Pages 82, 94–95: From *Spiritual Harvest* by Mary Lou Carney. Copyright © 1987 Abingdon Press. Used by permission of the author.

Pages 90–91: From *A Way Through the Wilderness* by Jamie Buckingham. Copyright © 1986. Used by permission of Jacqueline L. Buckingham.

Pages 98, 110, 157: From *Honesty, Morality & Conscience* by Jerry White. Copyright © 1979, 1986 NavPress. Revised and republished 1996. Used by permission.

Page 114: "Forgiveness" by Lucille Gardner. Used by permission of Stella A. Brown.

Page 124: From *Something More* by Catherine Marshall. Copyright © 1961 Chosen Books, a division of Baker Book House Company. Used by permission.

Page 135: From *How to Forgive Your Children* by Quin Sherrer with Ruthanne Garlock. Copyright © 1989 Aglow Publications, Lynwood, WA. Used by permission of the authors.

Pages 156–157: From *The ABC's of Wisdom* by Ray Pritchard. Copyright © 1997 Moody Publishers. Used by permission.

Page 159: From *What Makes a Man?* by Bill McCartney. Copyright © 1992 Promise Keepers. Used by permission.

Page 160: From *Junior Girl Scouts Handbook.* Copyright © 1998. Used by permission of Girl Scouts of the United States of America.

Pages 162–163: From "Tornado of Bucs Hype Swirl Past a Quiet Pillar" by Mary Jo Melone. Copyright © 1997 *St. Petersburg Times.* Used by permission.

Acknowledgments

Page 170: From *Seven Promises of a Promise Keeper.* Copyright © 1999 Promise Keepers by W. Publishing, Nashville, TN. Used by permission. All rights reserved.

Page 215: From *Out of Solitude* by Henri J. M. Nouwen. Copyright © 1974 Ave Maria Press, Notre Dame, IN. Used by permission.

Page 233: From *Meeting God at Every Turn* by Catherine Marshall. Copyright © 1961 Chosen Books, a division of Baker Book House Company. Used by permission.

Page 239: From *Molder of Dreams* by Guy Rice Doud, a Focus on the Family book published by Tyndale House. Copyright © 1990 Guy Doud. Used by permission. All rights reserved. International copyright secured.

Page 239: From *Christy* by Catherine Marshall. Copyright © 1961 Chosen Books, a division of Baker Book House Company. Used by permission.

Page 308: From *Mothering By Heart* by Robin Jones Gunn. Copyright © 1996, 2002 Robin Jones Gunn. Used by permission of Multnomah Publishers, Inc.

Scripture quotations marked AMPLIFIED are taken from *The Amplified Bible,* Old Testament, copyright © 1965, 1987 by the Zondervan Corporation. *The Amplified New Testament,* copyright © 1954, 1958, 1987 by The Lockman Foundation. Used by permission.

Scripture quotations marked KJV are taken from *The Holy Bible, King James Version.* Copyright © 1977, 1984 Thomas Nelson, Inc., Publishers. Used by permission.

Scripture quotations marked LB are taken from *The Living Bible.* Copyright © 1971. Used by permission of Tyndale House Publishers, Inc. All rights reserved.

Scripture quotations marked THE MESSAGE are from *The Message.* Copyright © 1993, 1994, 1995 Eugene H. Peterson. Used by permission of NavPress Publishing Group.

Scripture quotations marked NAS are taken from *The Holy Bible, New American Standard* version. Copyright © 1977 Holman Bible Publishers. Used by permission. All rights reserved.

Scripture quotations marked NIV are taken from *The Holy Bible, New International Version.* Copyright © 1973, 1978, 1984 International Bible Society. Used by permission of Zondervan Publishing House. All rights reserved.

Scripture quotations marked NKJV are taken from the *New King James Version.* Copyright © 1979, 1980, 1982 Thomas Nelson, Inc. Used by permission. All rights reserved.

Scripture quotations marked NLT are taken from *The Holy Bible, New Living Translation.* Copyright © 1996. Used by permission of Tyndale House Publishers, Inc. All rights reserved.

Scripture quotations marked NRSV are taken from the *New Revised Standard Version* of the Bible. Copyright © 1989 Division of Christian Education of the National Council of the Churches of Christ in the USA. Used by permission. All rights reserved.

Scripture quotation marked *The Promise* are taken from *The Promise.* Copyright © 1995 Thomas Nelson Inc., Publishers. Used by permission.

Scripture quotations marked RSV are taken from the *Revised Standard Version.* Copyright © 1952 Thomas Nelson & Sons, Limited. Used by permission.

Contents

The Pursuit of Virtues

*L*iving in God's Graces: The Value of Virtue is a book that celebrates the goodness in people and examines those qualities that make a person virtuous. We all know people who are good, righteous, pure of heart, and of high character. There are religious terms to describe this type of person; we might call them "holy" or "a saint." We might say of such a person, "she is so good," or "he is a blessing," or we might even say, "she has been like an angel to me." That is the wonderful thing about these people—they affect all those with whom they come in contact.

In order to look at the many aspects of the different virtues in an organized way and to more easily discover the nature of true virtue, this

book is divided into 14 chapters, each covering one virtue. The chapters and the contents of each chapter have been, for the most part, arranged in an arbitrary fashion.

The virtues covered in this book overlap one another, and you will find that virtues work together in a person's life. There are, of course, additional qualities that could be considered aspects of these virtues, but those included here will at least provide a starting point for the character traits you will want to teach to your children and your grandchildren. You will no doubt also find yourself integrating these virtues more fully into your own life.

The pursuit of virtues — which some have called a matter of developing good habits, making right choices, or resisting temptation — is something that can be taken on by anyone. We don't have to be beautiful, rich, or famous to become more virtuous. And the path to more virtuous living leads to increased happiness and fulfillment. The pursuit of tangible and temporary pleasures, like possessions or position, leaves us feeling unsatisfied and craving for more. But going after the intangibles, which is the goal of a virtuous life, brings satisfaction and lasting benefits that not only affect us and the people around us but also our offspring for generations to come.

In reading this book, you will note that some of the people mentioned faced great adversity in building character and becoming more

virtuous. We hope that this will give you hope during your hard times and an understanding that the right choices made during those times are the building blocks of character and good living.

You will also discover as you read this book that no matter when in history or where in the world a virtue is displayed, virtues are never-changing. A person of faith in 17th-century Germany will have the same qualities as a person of faith in 21st-century America. The diverse personalities included in this book—from different walks of life, points in history, and places in the world—illuminate the universality and timelessness of virtuous living.

As you read of the men and women in this book, what you will notice about them is their goodness of heart. Jesus said, "A good man out of the good treasure of his heart brings forth good things" (Matthew 12:35 NKJV). May these good things presented here be an inspiration to you.

This book is not meant to be read from cover to cover. It can be opened up to any page just as the valuables in a treasure chest can be picked up arbitrarily and enjoyed. Feast your eyes, your mind, and your heart on the treasures found in this book. It is our hope that *Living in God's Graces* will bring many hours of reading pleasure and also be a challenge to your life.

Love

God's greatest attribute is love. Love describes who God is and how He feels about us — that He desires to be with us and have an eternal union with us. God commands that we love Him and one another. It is through loving Him that we discover how much we are loved by Him, and then we are able to pass that love on to others. Love is the soul's greatest need, and even our health is better when we know we are loved. Love brings security and calms us. Every other virtue has love at its foundation.

God Is Love

If God has touched us with His love, the result will be love flowing through us to others. When we realize the depth of His love, our hearts long to show that kind of love to those around us.

Dear friends, let us practice loving each other, for love comes from God and those who are loving and kind show that they are the children of God, and that they are getting to know him better. But if a person isn't loving and kind, it shows that he doesn't know God—for God is love. God showed how much he loved us by sending his only Son into this wicked world to bring to us eternal life through his death.... Dear friends, since God loved us as much as that, we surely ought to love each other too. For though we have never yet seen God, when we love each other God lives in us and his love within us grows ever stronger.

1 JOHN 4:7–9, 11–12 LB

Faith Connects Us to Love

God gives us faith as a means of getting in touch with His love. For once we have that love, we can pass it on to others.

Love is greater than faith, because the end is greater than the means. What is the use of having faith? It is to connect the soul to God. And what is the object of connecting man with God? That he may become like God. But God is Love. Hence, Faith, the means, is in order to Love, the end. Love, therefore, obviously is greater than faith. "If I have all faith, so as to remove mountains, but have not love, I am nothing."

HENRY DRUMMOND, *THE GREATEST THING IN THE WORLD*

God's Promise of Eternal Love

God's love is a sure thing that is always reaching out to us. This promise is cause for celebration.

For I am convinced that nothing can ever separate us from his love. Death can't, and life can't. The angels won't, and all the powers of hell itself cannot keep God's love away. Our fears for today, our worries about tomorrow, or where we are—high above the sky, or in the deepest ocean—nothing will ever be able to separate us from the love of God demonstrated by our Lord Jesus Christ when he died for us.

ROMANS 8:38–39 LB

God's Desire for Love

God's desire for love from us is not primarily for His benefit, but for ours. One of His deepest desires is that we know His love, and some-how when we take action to love Him, it is then we discover just how much He loves us.

God wants us to love Him,
not because He is greedy for love,
but because when we are devoted
to loving Him,
we get in touch with
His powerful,
everlasting
love for us.
When we do,
we cannot contain it,
and it overflows to others.

Drawing near to God for Love

We sometimes fear drawing close to God, who is the source of love. Yet, when we finally choose to draw near, what a wonderful discovery we make—we are loved completely.

For years
I was afraid
To approach You—
afraid You'd disapprove
        of me
or declare me
        "unacceptable."

When I finally sought
        You,
I discovered You were
        tender,
compassionate, loving.
Now instead of fear,
during my life's purest
        moments,
I feel secure,
embraced,
totally accepted—
and completely loved by
        You.

Love Tested and True

*God's commandments are guide-
lines for our lives. While all of the
commandments are important, do
you know if any one is the most
important? One lawyer asked Jesus.*

And one of them, a lawyer, asked
him a question to test him. "Teacher,
which commandment in the law is
the greatest?" [Jesus] said to him,
"'You shall love the Lord your God
with all your heart, and with all
your soul, and with all your mind.'
This is the greatest and first commandment. And a second is like it:
You shall love your neighbor as
yourself.

MATTHEW 22:35–39

*What a grand thing, to be loved!
What a grander thing still, to love!*

VICTOR HUGO

Love one another as I have loved you.

JOHN 15:12

Love Is Most Important

If we want to determine a list of our accomplishments, we need to put at the top of the list:"What is the quality of love in my life?" That's what God uses to measure our lives.

If I speak in the tongues of mortals and of angels, but do not have love, I am a noisy gong or a clanging cymbal. And if I have prophetic powers, and understand all mysteries and all knowledge, and if I have all faith, so as to remove mountains, but do not have love, I am nothing. If I give away all my possessions, and if I hand over my body so that I may boast, but do not have love, I gain nothing.

Love is patient; love is kind; love is not envious or boastful or arrogant or rude. It does not insist on its own way; it is not irritable or resentful; it does not rejoice in wrongdoing, but rejoices in truth. It bears all things, believes all things, hopes all things, endures all things.

Love never ends. But as for prophecies, they will come to an end; as for tongues, they will cease; as for knowledge, it will come to an end. For we know only in part, and we prophesy only in part; but when the complete comes, the partial will come to an end. When I was a child, I spoke like a child, I thought like a child, I reasoned like a child; when I became an adult, I put an end to childish ways. For now we see in a mirror, dimly, but then we will see face to face. Now I know only in part; then I will know fully, even as I have been fully known. And now faith, hope, and love abide, these three; and the greatest of these is love.

1 Corinthians 13:1–13 NRSV

Loving Obedience

When we love Jesus, how we should act becomes clear. Even when we feel tempted to do the less-than-loving thing, we can remember His love for us and follow His example.

Four-year-old Flora is the kind of kid who makes people glad just to be alive when they see her shining face. Strangers must look at her and think, "Today's a good day, after all." Flora is good at hugs and verbal affirmations. She takes time with people, looks deep into their eyes, and listens carefully to their responses.

Flora frequently bounces into Doris's office, full of energy and questions about God. One day Flora said, "I asked my dad what a minister does, and he said you teach about God." Doris nodded. "That's a big part of my job."

Flora looked serious. "I want to teach about God when I grow up." Doris hugged Flora. "Oh, Flora, you already do teach about God." "I do?" she asked. "Yes, you are so full of love and goodness, how can people not know God if they know you?" Doris answered.

Flora chortled with delight, then bounced out of Doris's office back to the nursery school playground. Doris sat, realizing the truth of what she had said to Flora: What a difference we can make to the world when our love shines out from us! Doris couldn't help but think that Jesus was the sort of person whose presence made ordinary people feel special; unreligious types want to know God; the unrighteous yearn for justice. His very life was an example of what it means to follow all the commandments.

And so, when he tells us, "If you love me, you will keep my commandments," we know that only by such obedience do we really show our love. Sure, there are difficult people we find hard to love. That's when we let Jesus' love through us until our own love develops. There will be situations where it would be easiest to fudge a bit on our calling. But our love for Jesus holds us to keep His commandments.

True Love

True love is not based on outer appearances. It goes deeper and is a matter of the heart. Sometimes love is tested to see if it is real. It's inspiring when someone passes the test!

One day when I was in Brooklyn, I saw a young man going along the street without any arms. A friend who was with me, pointed him out, and told me his story. When the war broke out he felt it to be his duty to enlist and go to the front. He was engaged to be married, and while in the army letters passed frequently between him and his intended wife.

After the battle of the Wilderness the young lady looked anxiously for the accustomed letter. For a little while no letter was received. At last one came in a strange hand. She opened it with trembling fingers, and read these words: "We have fought a terrible battle. I have been wounded so awfully that I shall never be able to support you. A friend writes this for me. I love you more tenderly than ever, but I release you from your promise. I will not ask you to join your life with the maimed life of mine." That letter was never answered. The next train that left, the young lady was on it. She went to the hospital. She found out the number of his cot, and she went down the aisle, between the long rows of the wounded men. At last she saw the number, and, hurrying to his side, she threw her arms around his neck and said: "I'll not desert you. I'll take care of you." He did not resist her love. They were married, and there is no happier couple than this one.

DWIGHT L. MOODY, *ANECDOTES AND ILLUSTRATIONS OF DWIGHT L. MOODY*

Love Letter

When loved ones are separated by distance or death, the heart grieves. Love letters help bridge the gap and make us feel a little closer to the ones we have lost. But they are only lost for now, not forever.

Dear Jeffrey,
There was something special about you from the beginning. I could not explain it. Perhaps it was the twinkle in your bright blue eyes or your zest for life. You were with us for such a short time, but Daddy and I loved you very much. We enjoyed every minute. Steve and Angie loved you too. We all miss you and wish you were with us, but the Good Shepherd gathered you into His gentle arms and took you to a better place. As I walk with the Lord each day, I know I am close to you. We'll see you later, Jeffrey. Then, we'll be together forever.
> I love you dearly,
> Mom

FRAN CAFFEY SANDIN, *SEE YOU LATER JEFFREY*

Many waters cannot quench the flame of love, neither can the floods drown it.

SONG OF SOLOMON 8:7 LB

Jesus Loves Everyone

Jesus loves the little
children
All the children of the
world.
Red and yellow, black
and white
They are precious in
His sight
Jesus loves the little
children of the
world.

REV. C. H. WOOLSTON

How Much Does God Love You?

How much does God love you?
He loves you enough to let you go.
He loves you enough to let you hit bottom.
He loves you enough to let you come back.
He loves us so much that he will run to meet you.
That's how much God loves you.

RAY PRITCHARD, *THE ROAD BEST TRAVELED*

Who Is My Neighbor?

God's love comes with open eyes, open arms, and an open heart. Can we take the risk of loving our neighbor with God's kind of love?

One day an expert on Moses' laws came to test Jesus' orthodoxy by asking him this question: "Teacher, what does a man need to do to live forever in heaven?"

Jesus replied, "What does Moses' law say about it?"

"It says," he replied, "that you must love the Lord your God with all your heart, and with all your soul, and with all your strength, and with all your mind. And you must love your neighbor just as much as you love yourself."

"Right!" Jesus told him. "*Do* this and *you* shall live!"

The man ... asked, "Which neighbors?"

Jesus replied with an illustration: "A Jew going on a trip from Jerusalem to Jericho was attacked by bandits. They stripped him of his clothes and money and beat him up and left him lying half dead beside the road.

"By chance a Jewish priest came along; and when he saw the man lying there, he crossed to the other side of the ride and passed him by. A Jewish Temple-assistant ... looked at him lying there, but then went on.

"But a despised Samaritan came along, and when he saw him, he felt deep pity. Kneeling beside him the Samaritan soothed his wounds with medicine and bandaged them. Then he put the man on his donkey and walked along beside him till they came to an inn, where he nursed him through the night. The next day he handed the innkeeper [money] and told him to take care of the man....

"Now which of these three would you say was a neighbor to the bandits' victim?"

The man replied, "The one who showed him pity."

Then Jesus said, "Yes, now go and do the same."

LUKE 10:25–37 LB

A Prayer for Love of Neighbor

When neighbors don't measure up to our expectations, we can go to God for a change of heart. With His example and assistance, we can love our neighbors as God wants us to.

Heavenly Father, out of love for me You have sent Jesus to be my Savior. I am thankful for that, and I want to show my love for You by loving my neighbor. Keep me from harming anyone by hand, mouth, heart, or mind. Help me to bear patiently the wrongs that others do to me. Grant me a forgiving heart that I may not try to gain revenge. Let no angry thoughts arise in my mind, and guard my tongue from angry words.

Fill my heart with love for my Savior that I may show love to others by being kind and helpful to them. Help me to be a good example to others, and use my good example to bring them to know Jesus. Guide all my thoughts, words, and actions that all my doings may bring honor and praise to Your name and good to my friends and neighbors. Take us all to heaven in Your own good time.

Grant these blessings for the sake of Jesus. Amen.

Teenagers Pray

There is no fear in love; but perfect love casts out fear.

1 John 4:18 NKJV

Loving the Unlovable

We are naturally drawn to beautiful, kind, loving people. Mature love knows how to love those who seem unlovable, those who seem incapable of giving us anything in return for our love. This kind of love is heaven's love.

It's not hard to love
those who sparkle —
the diamond people
in the world.
The real test of loving
is being able to love
those who are like
pieces of coal —
those diamonds
in the rough
who might get us dirty.
But if we love them
even so —
with enough positive pressure
from love,
one day
they'll be diamonds too!

Love the Wicked

God stretches our heart's capacity when He tells us to love our enemies. Loving them proves that we belong to God, for He loves everyone, no matter what they have done.

Love your enemies! Do good to them! Lend to them! And don't be concerned about the fact that they won't repay. Then your reward from heaven will be very great, and you will truly be acting as sons of God: for he is kind to the unthankful and to those who are very wicked.

LUKE 6:35 LB

Departed Love

*When we grieve for lost loved ones, we grieve for ourselves. Let us cele-
brate that those who have gone home to heaven now know the full
essence of God's true love.*

One day I was upon my knees, communing with God upon the subject
[of my wife's death], and all at once he seemed to say to me, "You love
your wife?" "Yes," I said. "Well, did you love her for her own sake, or
yourself? If you loved her for her own sake, why do you sorrow that she
is with me? Should not her happiness with me, make you rejoice instead
of mourn, if you loved her for her own sake? Did you love her," he
seemed to say to me, "for my sake? If you loved her for my sake, surely
you would not grieve that she is with me. Why do you think of your loss,
and lay so much stress upon that instead of thinking of her gain? Can
you be sorrowful, when she is so joyful and happy? If you loved her for
her own sake, would you not rejoice in her joy, and be happy in her
happiness?"

CHARLES FINNEY, *AN AUTOBIOGRAPHY*

Loving Like Jesus

Loving like Jesus is not something that happens automatically. It is not something that's easy or natural. It is learned through the trials of life.

Often I say, "I want to be like Jesus," or "I want to love like Jesus." Part of me believes it can happen easily. God can wave a magic wand of grace over my life, and suddenly I'll be like Jesus. Reality hit the other day when I remembered how Jesus is described in the Bible: "He was despised and rejected by men, a man of sorrows, and familiar with suffering" (Isaiah 53:3 NIV). If I truly want to love like Jesus, I must be willing to be despised and rejected, to be subjected to sorrow and suffering. This is training ground for loving like Jesus. Each time I respond with love when someone is unloving toward me, I take one step closer to loving like Jesus.

Recently I did something I believed was loving toward a person in trouble. But another person looking on decided what I had done was evil and unloving, and she made sure she told me so. How dare she tell me I was evil and unloving! I shouted a list of her own faults back to her, and I ridiculed her for her lack of expertise as a judge of my actions. I let her know I thought she was spiritually blind and relationally stupid.

How did I respond to her verdict of "you are unloving"? By being unloving. How did I respond to her determination that what I—and I believe God—called good, she called evil? With evil. I see how far I have to go to love like Jesus. Repeatedly He faced people who told Him the good He did was evil. He never responded in any other way but with love. Sometimes He spoke a truth in return that hurt the listener, but it was always done in a loving way.

Every day I face tests in love. If I respond in love as Jesus would, I pass. If I don't, I fail. Lord, today I ask that you give me enough grace to respond to rejection with love—just like you did.

∽Love That Builds Up

Real love brings out the best in us. It looks beyond our faults and sees what we can become. This poem reflects that nurturing kind of love.

Love

I love you,
Not only for what
    you are,
But for what I am
When I am with you.

I love you,
Not only for what
You have made of
    yourself,
But for what
You are making of me.

I love you
For the part of me
That you bring out;
I love you
For putting your hand
Into my heaped-up
    heart
And passing over
All the foolish, weak
    things
That you can't help
Dimly seeing there.
And for drawing out

Into the light
All the beautiful
    belongings
That no one else had
    looked
Quite far enough to
    find.

I love you because you
Are helping me to
    make
Of the lumber of my
    life
Not a tavern

But a temple;
Out of the works
Of my every day
Not a reproach
But a song.

I love you
Because you have
    done
More than any creed
Could have done
To make me good,
And more than any
    fate
Could have done
To make me happy.

You have done it
Without a touch,
Without a word,
Without a sign.
You have done it
By being yourself,
Perhaps that is what
Being a friend means,
After all.

ANONYMOUS

Love and Mercy

Even though we may call ourselves "loving," often we justify an action by saying, "he deserved that." When someone comes against us with evil and we respond with good, we are showing mercy.

There is a word that describes the gap between human love and the love of God. That word is *mercy.* Repeatedly in Scripture there is reference to God's mercy and loving kindness. The two go together like love and marriage. Someone has said that grace is God giving us what we don't deserve. Mercy is Him withholding what we do deserve. Because of the evil in us, God's law says we deserve death, but because of His great mercy, which was brought to a climax by Jesus' death on the cross, we can have life instead — eternal life. We did nothing to deserve it. It is given to us by an act of His mercy.

When we consider the breakdown of marriages and friendships and every other human relationship, it is because we are trying to give the other person what we believe he or she deserves. You hurt me, and therefore you deserve to be hurt, is our rationale. What our relationships lack is mercy. Human love is how we behave toward someone who is loving toward us. Mercy or divine love is how we behave when someone has been unloving toward us. Mercy is unnatural for human beings. It is natural for God. That is why His love is far greater than ours. Yet as we draw close to Him and desire to be like Him, a miracle can take place in our lives. We can have mercy on others as He has had mercy on us. Imagine the wonders that love and mercy can work if they flow freely through us to every person we come in contact with. Let us never forget the wonders of God's mercy toward us — that is the key to letting it flow to others.

Through God's Eyes

When we see our enemies from God's perspective, compassion follows, for He has seen the sorrows in their hearts that have caused them to behave in such a manner. He longs to reach out to these people and comfort them, and He sometimes uses our hands to do it.

One dark morning when ice was forming a halo around each street lamp, a feeble-minded girl two rows ahead of us soiled herself. A guard rushed at her, swinging her thick leather crop while the girl shrieked in pain and terror. It was always terrible when one of these innocent ones was beaten. Still the *Aufseherin* continued to whip her. It was the guard we had nicknamed "The Snake" because of the shiny dress she wore. I could see it now beneath her long wool cape, glittering in the light of the lamp as she raised her arm. I was grateful when the screaming girl at last lay still on the cinder street.

"Betsie," I whispered when The Snake was far enough away, "what can we do for these people? Afterward I mean. Can't we make a home for them and care for them and love them?"

"Corrie, I pray every day that we are allowed to do this! To show them that love is greater!"

And it wasn't until I was gathering twigs later in the morning that I realized that I had been thinking of the feeble-minded, and Betsie of their persecutors.

CORRIE TEN BOOM, *THE HIDING PLACE*

'Tis better to have loved and lost, Than never to have loved at all.

ALFRED, LORD TENNYSON,
"IN MEMORIAM"

To Love Brings Happiness

We reflect the goodness of God most when we love others. It is life's highest, and sometimes most difficult, goal.

Not long ago we sat by the bedside of a dying woman who had experienced every blessing that life had to offer. We asked her what had made her the happiest. She did not answer that it was husband, children, home, or position. She replied, "To love."

ALICE BISHOP KRAMER AND ALBERT
LUDLOW KRAMER,
I BRING YOU JOY

A Loving Friend

Friend, you give so much to me —
a listening ear
a soothing voice
a caring heart
a helping hand
a healing hug
a cheering smile.
Thanks for being a loving friend.

Love and Friendship

A healthy friendship enhances our lives. What a blessing to have someone who wants to share all our joys and sorrows. We should continually strive to be the kind of friend God would like us to be—and the kind of friend that we would like to have.

Love from friendship—this love
      leads to light,
to peace and to deep joy.
This love never harms people.
It does not possess for itself.
It leaves the other person free.
And when it finds expression
in physical tenderness,
it stays pure.
But when one person wants
to possess another for himself
      alone,
for his own satisfaction,
he destroys the person he thinks
      he loves.
And destroys the friendship.
True, you will never be capable
of a totally unselfish friendship.
But you must always keep trying.

PHIL BOSMANS, "LOVE AND FRIENDSHIP"

A friend loves at all times.

PROVERBS 17:17 NKJV

Greater love has no man than this, that a man lay down his life for his friends.

JOHN 15:13 RSV

Prayer of a New Bride

The love of a new bride is fresh and exciting toward her husband—this man of her dreams. God will honor the sincere prayer of a bride, young or old, to keep that love alive.

Never let it end, God,
never—please—
all this growing loveliness,
all of these
brief moments of
fresh pleasure—
never let it end.
Let us always
be a little
breathless at love's beauty;
never let us
pause to reason
from a sense of duty;
never let us
stop to measure
just how much to give;
never let us
stoop to weigh love;
let us live—
and live!
Please, God,
let our hearts kneel always,
Love their only master,
knowing the warm impulsiveness

of shattered alabaster.*
I know You can see things
the way a new bride sees,
so
never let it end, God,
never—please.

* Mark 14:3

RUTH BELL GRAHAM,
RUTH BELL GRAHAM'S COLLECTED POEMS

Measured by Love

We do not naturally love like God does, but we can desire to grow in demonstrating His love to others. Our Christian fervor can be measured by our desire to grow in love, in spite of the struggles we will undoubtedly encounter.

The growth of Christian life is to be measured by the growth of love; and love itself is to be measured in its progressive states by its restfulness, its undisturbed trust, its victory over every form of fear. The state of perfect loving is incompatible with distrust. When the heart is first awakened to affection, it is disturbed and agitated. It fluctuates with every shade of hope and fear alternately. It rushes from one extreme of confidence to the opposite of doubt. But this is only while it is filling. The heart beginning to love is like a bay into which the star-drawn tides are rushing. The waters come with violence. They stir up the sand and sediment. They dash and murmur on the edges of the shore. They whirl and chafe about the rocks, and the whole bay is agitated with strife and counterstrife of swirling waters, until they have nearly reached their height. Then, when great depth is gained, when the shores are full, when no more room is found for the floods, the bay begins to tranquillize itself, to clear

its surface; and effacing every wrinkle, and blowing out every bubble, and hushing every ripple along the shore, it looks up with an open and tranquil face into the sky, and reflects clearly the sun and moon that have drawn it thither. And so does the soul, while filling, whirl with disquiet, and fret its edges with wrinkles and eddies; but when it is filled with love, it rests and looks calmly up, and reflects the image of its God.

HENRY WARD BEECHER, *LIFE THOUGHTS*

Sometimes Love Means Letting Go

One of the hardest things about loving someone is when we must help-
lessly watch them make wrong decisions and learn life's lessons the hard
way. Every parent knows the ache of watching the children we love make
foolish choices.

Sometimes love hurts
especially when we see
        loved ones
heading for danger.
We call to them, "Watch
        out!"
We grab at them
and try to bring them back
to a safer place.
But they don't listen.
They break loose,
ignoring our warnings.
And we must stand
on safe ground
and let them go
to learn the hard way.
And if our love is enduring,
we stand with open arms
to welcome them back
when they finally decide —
I am finished with danger —
I must go home.
And if our love is true,
we do not hold to,
"I told you so,"
but "I love you —
even so."

Sacrificial Love

O. Henry's timeless story is about much more than beautiful hair combs and a platinum watch chain. It's about true love's willingness to give everything—even those things that are most treasured—for those we love.

"Jim, darling," she cried, "don't look at me that way. I had my hair cut off and sold it because I couldn't have lived through Christmas without giving you a present. It'll grow out again—you won't mind, will you? I just had to do it. My hair grows awfully fast. Say 'Merry Christmas!' Jim, and let's be happy. You don't know what a nice—what a beautiful nice gift I've got for you."

"You've cut off your hair?" asked Jim, laboriously, as if he had not arrived at that patent fact yet even after the hardest mental labor.

"Cut it off and sold it," said Della. "Don't you like me just as well, anyhow? I'm me without my hair, ain't I?"

Jim looked about the room curiously.

"You say your hair is gone?" he said, with an air almost of idiocy.

"You needn't look for it," said Della. "It's sold, I tell you—sold and gone, too. It's Christmas even, boy. Be good to me, for it went for you. Maybe the hairs of my head were numbered," she went on with a sudden serious sweetness, "but nobody could count my love for you. Shall I put the chops on, Jim?"

Out of his trance Jim seemed quickly to wake. He enfolded Della...

Jim drew a package from his overcoat pocket and threw it upon the table.

"Don't make any mistake, Dell," he said, "about me. I don't think there's anything in the way of a haircut or a shave or a shampoo that could make me like my girl any less. But if you'll unwrap that package you may see why you had me going a while at first."

White fingers and nimble tore at the string and paper. And then an ecstatic scream of joy; and then,

alas! a quick feminine change to hysterical tears and wails, necessitating the immediate employment of all the comforting powers of the lord of the flat.

For there lay The Combs—the set of combs, side and back, that Della had worshipped for long in a Broadway window. Beautiful combs, pure tortoise shell, with jeweled rims—just the shade to wear in the beautiful vanished hair. They were expensive combs, she knew, and her heart had simply craved and yearned over them without the least hope of possession. And now, they were hers, but the tresses that should have adorned the coveted adornments were gone.

But she hugged them to her bosom, and at length she was able to look up with dim eyes and a smile and say: "My hair grows so fast, Jim!"

And then Della leaped up like a little singed cat and cried, "Oh, oh!"

Jim had not yet seen his beautiful present. She held it out to him eagerly upon her open palm. The dull precious metal seemed to flash with a reflection of her bright and ardent spirit.

"Isn't it a dandy, Jim? I hunted all over town to find it. You'll have to look at the time a hundred times a day now. Give me your watch. I want to see how it looks on it."

Instead of obeying, Jim tumbled down on the couch and put his hands under the back of his head and smiled.

"Dell," said he, "let's put our Christmas presents away and keep 'em a while. They're too nice to use just at present. I sold the watch to get the money to buy your combs. And now suppose you put the chops on."

The magi, as you know, were wise men—wonderfully wise men—who brought gifts to the Babe in the manger. They invented the art of giving Christmas presents. Being wise, their gifts were no doubt wise ones, possibly bearing the privilege of exchange in case of duplication. And here I have lamely related to you the uneventful chronicle of two foolish children in a flat who most unwisely sacrificed for each other the greatest treasures of their house. But in a last word to the wise of these days let it be said that of all who give gifts these two were the wisest. Of all who give and receive gifts, such as they are wisest. Everywhere they are wisest. They are the magi.

O. HENRY, "THE GIFT OF THE MAGI"

Love, Marriage, and Romance

Thinking of our own needs comes naturally. Thinking of what others need is supernatural. Anyone who's been married knows that sensing the needs of our spouse is a skill worth developing.

We have to give conscious attention to sensing the other person's needs and extending ourself beyond our own needs to meet them. We may not be too good at it at first, but we become more skillful through practice. Love in any marriage whose romance provides excitement and thrills, is an art. Anyone who becomes an artist at anything does so by developing superior skill in performance. Romance would be constantly in our marriage if more of us were skillful in the fine art of love.

W. CLARK ELLZEY, *HOW TO KEEP ROMANCE IN YOUR MARRIAGE*

Passing on God's Love

God does not love us so that we can hoard His love for ourselves. He desires that we pass it on to others. By preaching the joy of His love, we improve the lives of those around us—and our own lives in the process.

Pass It On
It only takes a spark to get a fire
　　　going,
and soon all those around can
　　　warm up to its glowing;
That's how it is with God's love,
　　　once you've experienced
　　　it:
You spread His love to ev'ryone,
　　　you want to pass it on.

What a wondrous time is spring—
　　　when all the trees are
　　　budding,
The birds begin to sing, the flowers
　　　start their blooming;
That's how it is with God's love,
　　　once you've experienced it:
You want to sing, it's fresh like
　　　spring, you want to pass it
　　　on.

I wish for you, my friend, this
　　　happiness that I've
　　　found—
You can depend on Him, it
　　　matters not where you're
　　　bound;
I'll shout it from the mountain top,
　　　I want my world to know:
The Lord of love has come to me,
　　　I want to pass it on.

KURT KAISER

Love Yourself

Self-love has gotten the bad name of being the same thing as selfishness. If you cannot love yourself, however, it is practically impossible to love others. But how can you tell the difference between self-love and selfishness?

As individuals come to understand that the Creator God of the universe is their loving heavenly Father, they realize that they are lovable, *love-ly,* to the One whose opinion counts most of all. Realizing that you are considered worthy of receiving love makes it a lot easier to love yourself, which protects against a deflated view of self.

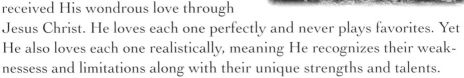

Still, this sense of being perfectly loved and having great significance in God's eyes must be seen in context, lest it be taken to an egotistical extreme. It must always be remembered that you are not an only child. If God lavished you, you would have on blinders that could easily make you have an overly inflated view of self.

God has many children who have received His wondrous love through Jesus Christ. He loves each one perfectly and never plays favorites. Yet He also loves each one realistically, meaning He recognizes their weaknessess and limitations along with their unique strengths and talents.

Knowing that God loves in such a perfectly balanced way makes it easier for us to accept ourselves, warts and all. If He who understands us better than we understand ourselves can still love us unconditionally, we certainly can learn to love ourselves. The all-knowing and all-wise God would never waste His love on someone who wasn't worth it. Some of us are better able to internalize His love and to love in return or in reflection of God's love.

Humility

*M*ost of us realize that we are naturally self-centered and that we
often respond to those around us in
ways that make us appear proud, haughty, or arrogant. But if we look at Jesus' life, we see an excellent
example of humil-
ity—an example
that we should strive
to follow. He taught
that pride was
destructive, but
humility was power-
ful. Rather than
touting His own
greatness, Jesus was
willing to kneel down
and wash the feet of
others, to show that
we all should be
servants to each
other—and to God.

Humility, that low, sweet root
From which all heavenly virtues shoot.

THOMAS MOORE

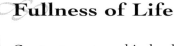

Fullness of Life

Contentment, and indeed usefulness, comes as the infallible result of great acceptances, great humilities — of not trying to make ourselves this or that, but of surrendering ourselves to the fullness of life — of letting life flow through us.

DAVID GRAYSON

He has showed you, O man, what is good.
And what does the Lord require of you?
To act justly and to love mercy
and to walk humbly with your God.

MICAH 6:8 NIV

But all who humble themselves before the Lord shall be given every blessing, and shall have wonderful peace.

PSALM 37:11 LB

Clothe yourselves with humility toward one another, for God is opposed to the proud, but gives grace to the humble. Humble yourselves, therefore, under the mighty hand of God, that He may exalt you at the proper time.

1 PETER 5:5–6 NAS

Understanding Humility

Like a multifaceted stone, the humble person's colors shine forth. By their nature, they are able to bear an injustice without retaliating, do one's duty even when one is not watched, keep at the job until it is finished, and make use of criticism without being defeated by it.

At one time true humility was thought to mean thinking negatively of oneself or belittling oneself. But this is neither a correct interpretation nor a current definition. It is more accurate to look at humility as not thinking more highly of ourselves than we ought to think: "Be honest in your estimate of yourselves, measuring your value by how much faith God has given you" (Romans 12:3 NLT).

Humility actually means not thinking of oneself, but putting others first. We disregard our rights and ambitions so we can serve God by serving others. Arriving at a place of humility is a result of understanding the biblical advice to "serve each other with humble spirits, for God gives special blessings to those who are humble, but sets himself against those who are proud. If you will humble yourselves under the mighty hand of God, in his good time he will lift you up" (1 Peter 5:5–6 LB).

The major obstacle to humility is pride. Pride and self-will become hindrances to our life of faith when we believe that God either does not care about or does not understand our situations in life. Or we believe that we don't need God's help to live our Christian life—we think we can look out for ourselves. When pride lures us into living independent of God, the result can be disastrous. The Book of Proverbs is full of warnings about the danger of allowing pride to creep into our lives: "Pride leads to arguments; be humble, take advice and become wise" (Proverbs 13:10 LB). "Pride ends in destruction; humility ends in honor" (Proverbs 18:12 LB).

A Humble Habit

Sometimes the best way to humble ourselves is just to walk outside and see everything God has created. A daily walk provides a peaceful way to focus on the world outside ourselves.

It is not always easy to simply step aside into solitude and rest and quietness. But unless I learn how, my entire growth in God will be endangered.

As a simple first step in this direction may I suggest the reader take twenty minutes each day to go out and walk alone—a brisk walk—only smiling to strangers—deliberately looking for the beauty and handiwork of God in the natural world about him, and inwardly adoring the Lord for who He is. Leave the worries and work at home or in the office. It will prove to be a tonic, a rest that results in growth in God.

Most of us have never learned the humble though powerful practice of concentrating on Christ. Outside, walking alone, away from the usual surroundings which remind us of our feverish workaday world, we can give our hearts a chance to center their interest and affection on Him.

W. PHILLIP KELLER, *As a Tree Grows*

A Prayer for Humility

*Only a life of prayer can help the believer
arrive at a spirit of humility, meekness, and
Christlikeness.*

I am praying, blessed Savior,
To be more and more like thee;
I am praying that thy Spirit
Like a dove may rest on me.

I am praying, blessed Savior,
For a faith so clear and bright
That its eye will see thy glory
Thro' the deepest, darkest night.

I am praying to be humbled
By the power of grace divine,
To be clothed upon with
        meekness,
And to have no will but thine.

I am praying, blessed Savior,
And my constant prayer shall be
For a perfect consecration,
That shall make me more like thee.

Chorus:
Thou who knowest all my weakness,
Thou who knowest all my care,
While I plead each precious
        promise,
Hear, oh, hear and answer prayer.

FANNY J. CROSBY

The Secret of Rest

Rather than proudly striving to get ahead on our own, we must learn to relax in the provision God has made for us. Only this will bring us God's peaceful rest.

Try to see the relation between meekness and restfulness. Many speak of humility as the secret of rest. You will not have rest while you are proud, neither will you have it just because you try your best to be humble. This may make life all the harder. It is only as you come to Jesus that you will find rest, and you will never come to Him as you believe Him proud instead of humble. Pride separates. You must come to Him as the meek and lowly One, believing Him to be such. 'Tis human to be proud; 'tis Godlike to be humble. You must see it in this way. Jesus can rest you because He is meek. Pride causes one to think of self. One has time for thought of others when he has little need of thought of self. Perhaps you have heard that the best way to rid yourself of a burden is to seek to bear another's burden; that to take upon you the yoke of another, means to be rid of your own yoke. But you can do this in a way that will cure your misery or add to it. Another's yoke may be far heavier than yours, and yet bearing it may rest you. Bearing it may add to your strength, while bearing your own weakens you.

Jesus' yoke and burden is that of others. He cannot have burdens of His own, for He is without pride. Reputation Jesus did not care about, for He made Himself of no reputation. Riches of earth He did not covet, so loss of money could not affect him. He could not be troubled by outward losses; to Him there could not be loss in these. Some care for one thing for self, some for another; He cared for nothing, and so He was care-free. This is noble living. The truly great are the truly meek. They must be so.

DAVID C. COOK, *REST; OR, THE SONG OF LOVE*

Jesus Humbled Himself

Christ was the perfect example of what being humble really means. While it may be difficult, we should make every effort to follow His example of humility.

Don't be selfish; don't live to make a good impression on others. Be humble, thinking of others as better than yourself. Don't just think

about your own affairs, but be interested in others, too, and in what they are doing.

Your attitude should be the kind that was shown us by Jesus Christ, who, though he was God, did not demand and cling to his rights as God, but laid aside his mighty power and glory, taking the disguise of a slave and becoming like men. And he humbled himself even further, going so far as actually to die a criminal's death on a cross.

Yet it was because of this that God raised him up to the heights of heaven and gave him a name

which is above every other name, that at the name of Jesus every knee shall bow in heaven and on earth and under the earth, and every tongue shall confess that Jesus Christ is Lord, to the glory of God the Father.

PHILIPPIANS 2:3–11 LB

The Secret of True Humility

The Apostle Paul was deeply humble. He knew he had worked hard and accomplished much, but only because God had poured kindness and grace upon him. True humility is not convincing yourself that you are worthless, but recognizing God's work in you. It is having God's perspective on who you are and acknowledging his grace in developing your abilities.

LIFE APPLICATION BIBLE NOTES (1 CORINTHIANS 15:9 LB)

Humble yourselves in the sight of the Lord, and he shall lift you up. J AMES 4:10 KJV

The humble shall see their God at work for them. No wonder they will be so glad! All who seek for God shall live in joy.

PSALM 69:32 LB

Judging Is Not up to Us

For some reason, we tend to evaluate other people. Yet it's not our job to judge others. That remains the work of God.

Have you ever noticed how often we make snap judgments about people we hardly know? We catch a glimpse of a person and suddenly feel able to judge them. Most often, if we can take time to get to know that person, we realize that our first impressions were, at best, superficial; at worst, dead wrong.

Perhaps it is human nature to judge. Most people have at least a small core of insecurity that comes out in the need to compare.

More insidious is our need to judge the heart and soul of another person. "She's only doing this to get ahead." "He's a stingy person." "She wouldn't offer help if it would save her life." "He's not a very ethical person." "I wouldn't trust him farther than I could throw him." "Have you ever met somebody so irresponsible?"

Jesus cuts to the chase on our need to stand in judgment of others. Our limited human experience does not give us the perspective or right to pass judgment on others. If judgment needs to happen, we can be sure that God will take care of it.

The next time you feel self-righteous judgment welling up inside you, try to catch yourself and analyze from where the need to judge is coming. Are you threatened by the other person? Feeling insecure about some aspect of your life? Do you need to stand out in the crowd? Our need to judge usually says more about us than about the person we're judging.

It is better to be of a humble spirit with the lowly, Than to divide the spoil with the proud.

PROVERBS 16:19 NAS

Humility vs. Pride

There is an appropriate time to have pride in our accomplishments as well as a time to be humble.

In God's scale of values, humility stands very high. He has always loved to advance the humble. Such a quality should be ever growing.

Paul acknowledged in 1 Corinthians 15:9, "I am the least of the apostles, that am not meet to be called an apostle" (KJV). Another time he was able to boast, "I have fought a good fight" (2 Timothy 4:7). So there is the right kind of pride, but it is always tempered by humility.

TED W. ENGSTROM, *THE MAKING OF A CHRISTIAN LEADER*

No More, No Less

What does humility really mean? It doesn't mean you should look down on yourself, but that you should accept yourself for who you are, including the good and the bad.

I had long misunderstood humility. Thinking it to be like an inferiority complex, I adopted a properly despondent look and asserted that I was nothing—I couldn't sing, couldn't preach, couldn't play the piano or any other instrument, was barely coordinated enough to walk. People would respond as expected by saying, "My, you are so humble." In all "humility" I would thank them for noticing.

Now, I realize that this attitude was not humility, it was sickness. Humility is no hang-dog approach to life. Humility is simply seeing ourselves as we actually are, not higher nor lower. It means being gut-level honest about ourselves—being up front. It means knowing who we are and owning that—and owning our emotions. It means living without hypocrisy.

GAYLE D. ERWIN, *THE JESUS STYLE*

Realistic Humble Confidence

When some people go fishing, they expect the fish to jump in the boat. When that doesn't happen, they give up quickly. What can you learn from impatient fishermen that is of eternal significance?

Fishing can be an exercise in frustration, especially if your ego is on the line. If your expectations are too high, if you have bragged about how many fish you will catch, or if you boasted about how big the fish you catch will be, the trip can turn out to be a meal of humble pie. It is different when you fish for a living . . . if you are going to make a living at fishing. The cocky and shortsighted don't last long as professional fishermen. They can't take the waiting and humbling.

On the other hand, there is a special kind of confidence that effective fishers possess. Even though they know that many factors impact the fishing, they also know that alertness, shrewdness, and perseverance usually pay off in the end. Over time, the large catches will be made, though sometimes in ways they don't expect.

Several of Jesus' closest followers, including Simon Peter and his brother, Andrew, were veteran fishermen. From long experience, they understood the patience and humility it takes to land fish. They did not comprehend, however, how to land a person by telling them about Jesus. They possessed neither the patience nor the humble confidence needed to be effective in that realm.

Jesus had watched them fish. He realized that fishing, in many respects, is like witnessing to other people. But the disciples didn't understand that. So while they possessed the proper humble confidence for fishing, they had no experience in telling others about Jesus. They tended to be either fearful or falsely confident. That seems to be why Jesus worded his call to Peter and Andrew the way he did. He knew that, in asking them to move from all they had ever known to the unknown, any parallels to fishing would make the call less fearful for them.

Fishing for people was indeed a perfect illustration for fishermen to relate to talking to people. Peter and Andrew were much more comfortable in dealing with fish than people. But things would change for the better. The same alert made them highly effective fishers of people.

As apostles, Peter and Andrew, plus the other professional fishermen James and John, saw thousands of people respond in faith as they shared their own faith in Jesus. They "reeled them in" with the same kind of humble, patient confidence with which they had fished the Sea of Galilee.

The rapid response of Simon and Andrew reveals a great deal about how they felt about future success. They left with Jesus immediately, not because they hated fishing, but because they knew that fishing for people was the wise way to invest the humble confidence they had learned.

*True humility
and respect for the
Lord lead a man to
riches, honor and
long life.*

PROVERBS 22:4 LB

True Humility

True humility is viewing ourselves as we really are from God's perspective and acting accordingly. People today practice false humility when they talk themselves down so that others will think they are spiritual. False humility is self-centered; true humility is God-centered.

LIFE APPLICATION BIBLE NOTES
(COLOSSIANS 2:18 LB)

Humility Is My Aim

"So our aim is to please him always in everything we do" (2 Corinthians 5:9 LB).

My aim is to please Him through
    communing in prayer;
  to show His love and for others care;
  to read His Word as my guide for life;
  to cease my grumbling that causes strife;
  to be open to God's leading and His
    will;
  to take time to meditate, be quiet,
    and still;
  to continually grow in my Christlike
    walk; and
  to be more like Jesus in my life and my
    talk.

Faith

To have faith is to believe, to trust, to have confidence in, or to rely on something or someone. Faithfulness describes the quality of someone with unswerving allegiance to an oath or a promise. Our example of faithfulness comes from a God who has kept and is in the process of keeping every promise contained in the Scriptures. We are commanded to "have faith in God," and out of that faith flows our ability to remain faithful to people—to keep the promises we have made as husbands and wives, as parents and children, and as servants of God.

It is never a question with any of us of faith or no faith; the question always is, "In what or in whom do we put our faith?"

ANONYMOUS

Faith never knows where it is being led, but it loves and knows the One Who is leading.

OSWALD CHAMBERS, *MY UTMOST FOR HIS HIGHEST*

The Object of True Faith

Faith thrives when we stay focused on God rather than on ourselves.

Faith is the least self-regarding of the virtues. It is by its very nature scarcely conscious of its own existence. Like the eye which sees everything in front of it and never sees itself, faith is occupied with the Object upon which it rests and pays no attention to itself at all. While we are looking at God we do not see ourselves—blessed riddance. The man who has repeated failures will experience real relief when he stops tinkering with his soul and looks away to the perfect One. While he looks at Christ the very things he has so long been trying to do will be getting done within him. It will be God working in him to will and to do.

Faith is not in itself a meritorious act; the merit is in the One toward Whom it is directed. Faith is a redirecting of our sight, a getting out of the focus of our own vision and getting God into focus.

A. W. TOZER, *THE PURSUIT OF GOD*

Even the Smallest Faith

Believing and acting on your beliefs are important parts of faith. Jesus commends us for what seem like small acts or humble words. God transforms what we offer into hope for the world.

When Jemma's children were very young, one of their favorite books was *The Little Engine That Could*. It was the story of a small train engine that admired all the big locomotive engines in the train yard but never got asked to do any significant work. Jemma doesn't remember the reason, but one day the train gets asked to take goodies for boys and girls up a big hill. The words the train says as it huffs and puffs up the hill are, "I think I can." Over and over, the little engine repeats the chant until it succeeds in cresting the hill and then descends to a cheering crowd of boys and girls—and with Jemma's children cheering, too.

"I think I can" was one of the first notions of faith for Jemma's children. Size was not the important ingredient—but rather belief and desire. When Jemma's children read the story of little David

and the giant Goliath in the Bible, they learned again that size was not the key; it was David's belief that God was with him and his knowledge that he was very good with a slingshot.

Faith does not have to be grand, complete, big, or perfect. Faith is the willingness to believe, to trust that something can happen, so we give ourselves over to the effort. Faith for the Christian is the willingness to step out in confidence that there is a God. Faith is believing that God cares about us and is with us in all our efforts.

Jesus is encouraging the disciples to have faith, to trust a little deeper, to have the confidence that with God all things are possible. He uses two images that would be familiar to his listeners. Though mustard seeds are not the smallest seeds, it was common to use them as an illustration of smallness. Jesus is encouraging the disciples' belief and confidence in this way. Keep trusting. Keep loving. Keep praying. You don't have to have it all figured out. Take one more step—a small step even.

In Hebrew circles, great teachers would often use the image of moving mountains as a way of encouraging listeners to overcome difficulties. Jesus chooses this second image, moving mountains, to point out to and encourage the disciples that the hardest tasks of life can be accomplished with the smallest of faith. What seems insurmountable and impossible, mountain-big, can be overcome by even a little faith.

One word or one act can cause all sorts of things to happen. Something that seems insignificant can make a huge difference. One visit to a worship service can start a person on the journey of faith. One teacher can make the difference for a student. One mountain-top experience or religious revival can call a person to a new vocation. One senseless tragedy can spur a community to open a teen center. One candle lit in the darkness can chase away the dark.

In December 1955, Rosa Parks was tired from working all day and was glad for a seat on the bus going home. When some white people got on the bus, Rosa was asked to move to the back with the rest of the blacks. She refused, and her arrest motivated the blacks in Montgomery, Alabama, to call for a bus boycott. The person chosen to lead the boycott was a young pastor named Martin Luther King, Jr. One person's small act can catalyze a new "I think I can" movement for social change.

God can take our smallest acts, our seemingly insignificant words, and use them for good. We can turn our best efforts over to God and trust that they fit into God's plan for justice and peace, healing and unity upon Earth.

Steps for Growing in Faith

If we want to grow in faith, we must cooperate with God. Doing our part is the key to growing in faith. Getting to know Him and His ways will enable us to "see" what He is asking us to do.

For as you know him better, he will give you, through his great power, everything you need for living a truly good life: he even shares his own glory and his own goodness with us! And by that same mighty power he has given us all the other rich and wonderful blessings he promised; for instance, the promise to save us from the lust and rottenness all around us, and to give us his own character.

But to obtain these gifts, you need more than faith; you must also work hard to be good, and even that is not enough. For then you must learn to know God better and discover what he wants you to do. Next, learn to put aside your own desires so that you will become patient and godly, gladly letting God have his way with you. This will make possible the next step, which is for you to enjoy other people and to like them, and finally you will grow to love them deeply. The more you go on in this way, the more you will grow strong spiritually and become fruitful and useful to our Lord Jesus Christ. But anyone who fails to go after these additions to faith is blind indeed, or at least very shortsighted, and has forgotten that God delivered him from the old life of sin so that now he can live a strong, good life for the Lord.

2 PETER 1:3–9 LB

More Precious Than Gold

If our faith was never tested, how would we know we had any? When things go wrong and we can still say, "I believe in God no matter what happens," we show our faith to be real.

These trials are only to test your faith, to see whether or not it is strong and pure. It is being tested as fire tests gold and purifies it — and your faith is far more precious to God than mere gold; so if your faith remains strong after being tried in the test tube of fiery trials, it will bring you much praise and glory and honor on the day of his return.

1 PETER 1:7 LB

Without faith, we are as stained glass windows in the dark.

ANONYMOUS

The Testing of Faith

Faith sometimes means giving back to God the things and people we cherish most.

Later on, God tested Abraham's [faith and obedience]....

"Take with you your only son—yes, Isaac whom you love so much—and go to the land of Moriah and sacrifice him there as a burnt offering upon one of the mountains which I'll point out to you!"

The next morning Abraham..., his son Isaac and two young men who were his servants... started off to the place where God had told him to go. On the third day of the journey Abraham saw the place in the distance.

"Stay here with the donkey," Abraham told the young men, "and the lad and I will travel yonder and worship, and then come right back."

Abraham placed the wood for the burnt offering upon Isaac's shoulders, while he himself carried the knife and flint for striking a fire. So the two of them went on together.

"Father," Isaac asked, "we have the wood and flint to make

the fire, but where is the lamb for the sacrifice?"

"God will see to it, my son," Abraham replied....

When they arrived at the place where God had told Abraham to go, he built an altar and placed the wood in order, ready for the fire, and then tied Isaac and laid him on the altar over the wood. And Abraham took the knife and lifted it up to plunge it into his son, to slay him.

At that moment the Angel of God shouted to him from heaven, "Abraham! Abraham!"

"Yes, Lord!" he answered.

"Lay down the knife; don't hurt the lad in any way," the Angel said, "for I know that God is first in your life—you have not withheld even your beloved son from me."

Then Abraham noticed a ram caught by its horns in a bush. So he took the ram and sacrificed it, instead of his son, as a burnt offering on the altar....

Then the Angel of God called again to Abraham from heaven. "I, the Lord, have sworn by myself that because you have obeyed me and have not withheld even your beloved son from me, I will bless you with incredible blessings... all because you have obeyed me."

GENESIS 22:1–18 LB

Obstacles to Faith

When a task requiring faith confronts us, voices around us may say, "It can't be done." The voice may even come from within us, and we may want to quit before we start. But if we hold on to faith, we can succeed, no matter what the critics say.

It Couldn't Be Done

Somebody said that it couldn't be done,
But he with a chuckle replied
That "maybe it couldn't" but he would be one
Who wouldn't say so till he'd tried.
So he buckled right in with the trace of a grin
On his face. If he worried he hid it.
He started to sing as he tackled the thing
That couldn't be done, and he did it.

Somebody scoffed: "Oh, you'll never do that;
At least no one ever has done it";
But he took off his coat and he took off his hat,
And the first thing we knew he'd begun it.
With a lift of his chin and a bit of a grin,
Without any doubting or quiddit,
He started to sing as he tackled the thing
That couldn't be done, and he did it.

There are thousands to tell you it cannot be done,
There are thousands who prophesy failure;
There are thousands to point out to you one by one,
The dangers that wait to assail you.
But just buckle in with a bit of a grin,
Just take off your coat and go to it;
Just start in to sing as you tackle the thing
That "cannot be done," and you'll do it.

EDGAR GUEST, *THE PATH TO HOME*

Faith Brings Rewards

Some people blame their lack of faith on their difficult circumstances. Yet rough situations are often the catalysts for displays of great faith.

We live by faith, not by sight. — 2 CORINTHIANS 5:7 NIV

In 1949 the trustees of Rollins College in Winter Park, Florida, asked Mary to accept an honorary degree.

Mary Bethune received the first honorary degree ever given to a Negro by a white southern college.

She stood as tall as she could as she listened to President Holt say, "Mary McLeod Bethune, I deem it one of the highest privileges that has come to me as President of Rollins College to do honor to you this morning. I am proud that Rollins is, I am told, the first white college in the South to bestow an honorary degree on one of your race. You have in your own person demonstrated that from the humblest beginnings and through the most adverse circumstances it is still possible for one who has the will, the intelligence, the courage, and the never-failing faith in God and in your fellow man to rise from the humblest cabin in the land to a place of honor and influence among the world's eminent."

ELLA KAISER CARRUTH, *SHE WANTED TO READ: THE STORY OF MARY MCLEOD BETHUNE*

For the Lord loves the just and will not forsake his faithful ones.

PSALM 37:28 NIV

A Mother of Faith

Sometimes a person doesn't have much faith in himself, but a loved one has faith enough to fill in the gaps.

Who could have believed that the worst student in Higgins Elementary School fifth grade would one day become a world-famous brain surgeon? That a poor ghetto kid would learn to perform operations too risky for some of the most highly trained surgeons to attempt? That the kid who got zero out of thirty on his math quizzes would regularly snatch the lives of tiny children from the edge of death?

Mother believed. She told me many times, "If you ask the Lord for something and believe he will do it, then it'll happen." My life is living proof that it's true.

BEN CARSON, M.D., *BEN CARSON*

Faith Dreams Big

In 1976, Millard Fuller and his wife founded Habit for Humanity, which has assisted in constructing around 60,000 homes for low-income families around the world.

I often say that there is a difference between faith and foolishness. We want to challenge people to get as close to foolishness as they can . . . without crossing the line. Think creatively and boldly! Go ahead and set a date! With God, all things are possible.

MILLARD FULLER, *A SIMPLE, DECENT PLACE TO LIVE*

Learning About Faith from Children

When someone, especially an expert, predicts the worst, we tend to believe them. It takes a dynamic faith to believe something different—to believe that God can and will intervene in the situation.

"Let's pray together for Riffy," I said to my daughter, Tami, who was six years old.

I took our frail cat into my arms and stroked his caramel-colored fur. The doctor had told us there was no hope. The unknown infection, unresponsive to medication, was taking over Riffy's body. His fever remained high, his appetite low. The doctor said we could bring him home, but the symptoms would worsen. Then we could bring him back to be put to sleep.

I prepared in my mind a prayer about helping Tami deal with his inevitable death.

But before I could get my prayer out, Tami began, "Oh God, we know You have great power. Please make Riffy all better, because he is my best friend."

Now we have a problem, I thought. I tried to say the prayer I had planned about preparing for Riffy's death, but Tami would have none of it.

"God is going to make Riffy well, Mommy," she insisted. "I know He wouldn't take my best friend away from me."

How could I explain to her that God did not always heal? How could I explain God's sovereign plan, which we did not always understand? How could I explain the statement, "If it be Thy will?"

I did not argue with her. I marveled at her faith. Worrisome thoughts about what was going to happen when Riffy's condition worsened nagged at me.

"Don't worry, Mom—Riffy will get better soon," she assured me.

Riffy did get well. The day after Tami's prayer, he started eating again. Purring and playing came next, and before long Riffy was back to his frisky self again. Once again he hid under Tami's bed to pounce out and bite our toes. He chased rodents in the yard. And he resumed his regular adventure of climbing the tall pine tree in our backyard.

The only one who wasn't amazed by Riffy's recovery was Tami. She'd had faith all along.

Coping by Faith

By faithfully turning to God in times of loss and grief, we discover that He can be depended upon to carry us through. Dave Dravecky, a former pitcher for the San Francisco Giants, recounts the loss of his arm to cancer and the faith that got him through the ordeal.

I'm not getting through the loss of my arm because I am a great coper. I'm getting through it because I have a Father in heaven who is a great giver. He is where I find grace. At the time I need strength, he puts it in my heart or provides it through someone who is close to me, whether that's a family doctor or simply a friend. I don't earn it. I don't deserve it. I don't bring it about. It's a gift.

DAVE AND JAN DRAVECKY, *WHEN YOU CAN'T COME BACK*

Now faith is being sure of what we hope for and certain of what we do not see.

HEBREWS 11:1 NIV

Walking on Water

*It's amazing what we can accom-
plish if we keep our eyes off our
circumstances and on the One who
is in control of them.*

Sometimes I'm like Peter,
and I walk on water.
I stand above my circumstances,
which are like the swirling
        tempests of the sea.
But then, like Peter,
I take my eyes off Jesus
and concentrate on things below.
Soon I start to sink.
How I long to have
a consistent
water-walking
eyes-on-Jesus
faith.

*I've been driven
many times to my
knees by the
overwhelming
conviction that I had
nowhere else to go.*

ABRAHAM LINCOLN, *THE WIT & WISDOM OF
ABRAHAM LINCOLN*

Faith Finds a Way

Some people view obstacles as dead ends. Others conclude that those same obstacles are merely cleverly disguised opportunities. What makes the difference between these opposite outlooks?

Conventional wisdom says, "Where there's a will, there's a way." But spiritual wisdom, the kind that comes from Jesus, takes an extra, necessary step. Where's there's a will, there's the ability to choose to trust. And where there's trust in the Lord, there's a way!

A classic example of this kind of faith was seen when four people brought a paralyzed man to Jesus to be healed. The crowd that had come to see Jesus was so thick that the people with the paralytic couldn't get into the building where Jesus was. The huge crowd would have been enough to convince most people to give up and go home.

But these four were not most people. They firmly believed Jesus could heal their paralyzed loved one, and they were determined to find a way to get him to Jesus.

Still, there was no way in through the conventional entrances. But why limit the options to conventional ones? These men of faith decided to go up the outside stairs and open a hole in the flat tile or clay roof of the building. Through the opening, they lowered down the paralytic directly into the presence of Jesus.

Almost anyone else would have been shocked at the nerve of this plan to crash the party, right through the roof. Jesus, instead, was moved by the faith that motivated this extraordinary, creative approach. He did not scold the invaders. He commended them for their faith and extended the eternal gift of forgiveness.

Almost everyone encounters obstacles in their lives on a fairly consistent basis. The real question is, "Do you see them as insurmountable obstacles or challenging opportunities?"

Go to God

It helps God know what we want when we ask Him for the things we desire. Those things need not be material.

Lord, give me faith that tries and tests the things unseen, and assures itself of thee who art the truth, that doubt may not overwhelm, nor darkness cover me; give me hope, that I may follow the light of thy sure promises, and lose not the way nor fall into byways; give me love, that I may give thee myself as thou givest; for thou, O Lord God, art the thing that I long for; and thou art blessedness beyond all thought and heart's desiring.

FREDERICK MACNUTT

*No matter what my ears may hear
Or what my eyes may see,
There's nothing for me to fear, Lord;
You're always here with me.*

Faith Keeps Its Eyes on God

David never mentions the size of the giant Goliath or how vicious he looks. What he does focus on is how faithful God has been in the past. He fully believes that God will see him through again. And He does!

Then Saul said to David, "You are not able to go against this Philistine to fight with him; for you are but a youth while he has been a warrior from his youth."

But David said to Saul, "Your servant was tending his father's sheep. When a lion or a bear came and took a lamb from the flock, I went out after him and attacked him, and rescued it from his mouth; and when he rose up against me, I seized him by his beard and struck him and killed him.

"Your servant has killed both the lion and the bear; and this uncircumcised Philistine will be like one of them, since he has taunted the armies of the living God."

And David said, "The Lord who delivered me from the paw of the lion and from the paw of the bear, He will deliver me from the hand of this Philistine."

Thus David prevailed over the Philistine with a sling and a stone, and he struck the Philistine and killed him; but there was no sword in David's hand.

1 SAMUEL 17:33–37, 50 NASB

Fear Versus Faith

We respond to stresses in our lives with either fear or faith. Fear is a great threat to our faith. That's why we often read in the Scriptures the directive: "Fear not." The closer we draw to God, the more our fears diminish.

Jesus lived at complete liberty. The poise of his life, his absolute command of himself, his capacity to confront every exigency of his career with calm, wise, unworried, unhasting discrimination, was due to his entire independence of fear.

Not meaning, either, that he had arrived at some static position where he was forever unassailable by the various threats which life holds over every man. The general upkeep of his mood of fearlessness made certain demands. He was required to keep himself constantly in the confidence of his own source of spiritual supply. Once he was asked by a Samaritan woman where, in his opinion, was the best place to seek God. Some said, she remarked, that God was to be sought in the holy mountain; others, the Jews, said that God was to be found in the temple at Jerusalem. Jesus told her that the time would come when men would not attempt to give God a localized address.

Jesus was not distrustful of the temple, as a fine memorial to man's reverence. He saw the point of that and commended it. He, himself, visited the temple frequently, and found it worthwhile. But he had to have a closer contact with God than that, to keep himself empowered with spiritual forces. He couldn't be in the temple all the time; and yet he knew he had to be conscious of God all the time. So, he conceived the practice of *living in the presence of God.*

While aware of that contact, he was beyond the reach of fear — not fears considered item by item; but *fear.* And to the maintenance of that mood, it was imperative that he keep himself free of fear-concepts. If you will go through the recorded gospels with a blue pencil and underscore all admonitions he offered on the subject of eliminating fear from human thought, you may be amazed to discover how considerable an area of his teaching was comprehended by this counsel.

And not only was he constantly urging other people to be fearless, but he was careful to avoid the contamination of their fears. He was indignant when they came howling in a panic to hurl their cowardice at him. In the storm on the Sea of Galilee, he sleeps. So confident of his own independence of physical forces was he that it was no longer necessary for him to brace himself against fear. He slept through the storm. His disciples shake him awake. What was the matter with him, anyway? Here they were, frightened to death, and he was able to sleep. Apparently they wanted him to be frightened, too. It is not enough that they be scared. He must wake up and see how serious is this menace that has stampeded them.

"Oh ye of little faith!" How often that phrase was on his lips. "Why are ye fearful . . . oh ye of little faith?"

A few days before he met his tragedy, Jesus, with his disciples, spent some time on the seacoast, near Tyre. It was a brief vacation from the wearing drain of dealing, daily, with great crowds of needy people. One day,

without warning, Jesus announced that he was about to start back now, for Jerusalem. He would attend the Passover Feast. Aware of the enmities which, in Jerusalem, were being brought to a sharp focus, and would unquestionably strike at his Master on the occasion of a day of enthusiasm for the old orthodoxy, Simon Peter begged Jesus not to go. It was by no means safe. He didn't really have to go. Let him stay where he was out of the reach of his enemies. "This must not be," said Peter. Jesus pushed him aside — and not very gently, either. Peter was getting in the way — Peter with his cowardice; with his program of safety first. Jesus did not consider that an act of friendship at all. His idea of a helpful friend was someone who stimulated you to free yourself of fears; not someone who called attention to them.

Constantly, he was endeavoring to encourage other people in their faith and fearlessness.

LLOYD C. DOUGLAS, *THE LIVING FAITH*

An Explorer with Faith

It takes faith to go beyond what others know—to explore new ideas, to stand on our convictions that there is something more, and to trust that God has called us to discover it.

He had a fine presence, a convincing way with him, due, more than anything else, to his sincere, enthusiastic belief in his own ideas. By temperament he was strongly religious. The tenets of his faith were to him living realities which never ceased to inspire his conduct, and this spiritual fervor had now extended to his belief in the mission that lay before him of discovering the lands and the peoples on the other side of the Atlantic.

CLIFFORD SMYTH,
BUILDERS OF AMERICA: CHRISTOPHER COLUMBUS

Faith is knowing without seeing, believing without fully understanding, trusting without touching the One who is ever faithful.

Promises Faithfully Kept

Faith is more than believing in who God is. It's believing that He will keep His promises.

Faith is not just about believing in God. It's about believing He'll do what He says—that He'll keep every promise He's made in the Holy Bible. When we are faithful, like God, we keep the promises we make. And when we have faith in another person, we believe they will keep the promises they have made.

Faith is nurtured by love, as the flame in a lamp is nurtured by the oil.

MARTIN LUTHER, *DISCOURSE ON FREE WILL*

A Faithful Friend

Faithful friends stick by us both when we're happy and when we're hurting—when we are nice and when we are not so nice. They put our welfare above theirs. One of life's greatest assets is a faithful friend.

So she departed from the place where she was, and her two daughters-in-law with her; and they went on the way to return to the land of Judah.

And Naomi said to her two daughters-in-law, "Go, return each of you to her mother's house. May the Lord deal with you as you have dealt with the dead and with me.

"May the Lord grant that you may find rest, each in the house of her husband." Then she kissed them, and they lifted up their voices and wept.

And they said to her, "*No*, but we will surely return with you to your people."

But Naomi said, "Return, my daughters. Why should you go with me? Have I yet sons in my womb, that they may be your husbands?

"Return, my daughters! Go, for I am too old to have a husband. If I said I have hope, if I should even have a husband tonight and also bear sons, would you therefore wait until they were grown? Would you therefore refrain from marrying? No, my daughters; for it is harder for me than for you, for the hands of the Lord has gone forth against me."

And they lifted up their voices and wept again; and Orpah kissed her mother-in-law, but Ruth clung to her.

Then she said, "Behold, your sister-in-law has gone back to her people and her gods; return after your sister-in-law."

But Ruth said, "Do not urge me to leave you or turn back from following you; for where you go, I will go, and where you lodge, I will lodge. Your people shall be my people, and your God, my God."

RUTH 1:7–16 NASB

Faith is a firm and certain knowledge of God's benevolence toward us.

JOHN CALVIN

Those of us who are strong and able in the faith need to step in and lend a hand to those who falter, and not just do what is most convenient for us.

ROMANS 15:1 THE MESSAGE

Keeping the Faith

Growing older doesn't necessitate letting go of faith. Even though our bodies are getting older and our thinking may not be as sharp as it once was, God is still the same. We can always depend on Him.

There is another thing that we of middle life need to guard against, and that is the loss of early enthusiasms and ideals. The tendency of life's actualities is to sober and sometimes embitter. It is a difficult thing to experience trial and failure, to see the hollowness and shame, the trickery and cruelty of the social, commercial, political world, and not get cynical and skeptical—to lose, if not your faith in God, what is next worse, your faith in man and interest in man. It is hard, in contact with the actual world to preserve your faith in an ideal world, your ardor in its pursuit. The youthful vision fades, romance gives way to prosy plodding, and life's springtime grows into the hot, dusty parched summer. Oh, men and women of riper years, let us not fail to carry our earlier enthusiasms into the dry details, the grave responsibilities of later life and make the desert places rejoice and blossom as the rose!

CHARLES SUMNER HOYT, *THE OCTAVE OF LIFE*

The Faithful Old Woman

Having faith is believing that even small things have significance. People of faith believe that every person matters, that even one person can make a difference, and that God takes small things and makes them into great things.

An old woman who was seventy-five years old had a Sabbath-school two miles away among the mountains. One Sunday there came a terrible storm of rain, and she thought at first she would not go that day, but then she thought, "What if some one should go and not find me there?" Then she put on her waterproof, and took her umbrella and overshoes, and away she went through the storm, two miles away, to the Sabbath-school in the mountains. When she got there she found one solitary young man, and taught him the best she knew how all the afternoon. She never saw him again, and I don't know but the old woman thought her Sabbath-school had been a failure. That week the young man enlisted in the army, and in a year or two after the old woman got a letter from the soldier thanking her for  going through the storm that Sunday. This young man thought that stormy day he would just go and see if the old woman was in earnest, and if she cared enough about souls to go through the rain. He found she came and taught him as carefully as if she was teaching the whole school, and God made that the occasion of winning the young man to Christ. When he lay dying in a hospital he sent the message to the old woman that he would meet her in heaven. Was it not a glorious thing that she did not get discouraged because she had but one Sunday-school scholar? Be willing to work with one.

Dwight L. Moody, *Anecdotes and Illustrations of Dwight L. Moody*

People of Faith

The Bible is filled with stories of people who had faith—people who believed what God promised and acted on those beliefs.

By an act of faith, Abel brought a better sacrifice to God than Cain. It was what he *believed,* not what he *brought,* that made the difference. That's what God noticed and approved as righteous. After all these centuries, that belief continues to catch our notice.

By an act of faith, Enoch skipped death completely. "They looked all over and couldn't find him because God had taken him." We know on the basis of reliable testimony that before he was taken, "he pleased God." It's impossible to please God apart from faith. And why? Because anyone who wants to approach God must believe both that he exists *and* that he cares enough to respond to those who seek him.

By faith, Noah built a ship in the middle of dry land. He was warned against something he couldn't see, and acted on what he was told. The result? His family was saved. His act of faith drew a sharp line between the evil of the

unbelieving world and the rightness of the believing world. As a result, Noah became intimate with God.

By an act of faith, Abraham said yes to God's call to travel to an unknown place that would become his home. When he left he had no idea where he was going. By an act of faith he lived in the country promised him, lived as a stranger camping in tents. Isaac and Jacob did the same, living under the same promise. Abraham did it by keeping his eye on an unseen city with real, eternal foundations—the City designed and built by God.

By faith, barren Sarah was able to become pregnant, old woman as she was at the time, because she believed the One who made a promise would do what he said. That's how it happened that from one man's dead and shriveled loins there are now people numbering into the millions.

Each one of these people of faith died not yet having in hand what was promised, but still believing. How did they do it? They saw it way off in the distance, waved their greeting, and accepted the fact that they were transients in this world. People who live this way make it plain that they are looking for their true home. If they were homesick for the old country, they could have gone back any time they wanted. But they were after a far better country than that — *heaven* country. You can see why God is so proud of them, and has a City waiting for them.

By an act of faith, Isaac reached into the future as he blessed Jacob and Esau....

By an act of faith, Jacob on his deathbed blessed each of Joseph's sons in turn, blessing them with God's blessing, not his own — as he bowed worshipfully upon his staff.

By an act of faith, Joseph, while dying, prophesied the exodus of Israel, and made arrangements for his own burial.

By an act of faith, Moses' parents hid him away for three months after his birth. They saw the child's beauty, and they braved the king's decree.

By faith, Moses, when grown, refused the privileges of the Egyptian royal house. He chose a hard life with God's people rather

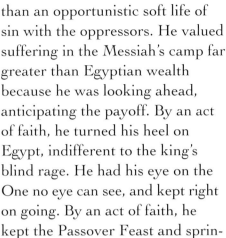

than an opportunistic soft life of sin with the oppressors. He valued suffering in the Messiah's camp far greater than Egyptian wealth because he was looking ahead, anticipating the payoff. By an act of faith, he turned his heel on Egypt, indifferent to the king's blind rage. He had his eye on the One no eye can see, and kept right on going. By an act of faith, he kept the Passover Feast and sprinkled Passover blood on each house so that the destroyer of the firstborn wouldn't touch them.

By an act of faith, Israel walked through the Red Sea on dry ground. The Egyptians tried it and drowned.

By faith, the Israelites marched around the walls of Jericho for seven days, and the walls fell flat.

By an act of faith, Rahab, the Jericho harlot, welcomed the spies and escaped the destruction that came on those who refused to trust God.

HEBREWS 11:4–16, 21–31 THE MESSAGE

God's Surprises

When we step out and do the thing we believe God wants us to do, even if it doesn't make sense, that's faith. Our greatest rewards can come from those acts.

Occasionally God surprises us by letting us find out how He used some word we spoke or action that we took years ago and perhaps forgot all about. About a century ago Stephen Grellat was led one day to go out to a heavily forested area of America to preach. It was a strong inward compulsion of the Holy Spirit. When he arrived at the loggers' camp, he found they had moved to another location, and their shanties were deserted. However, he was so sure he was sent by God that he went into an empty shanty and preached to the bare walls the sermon God had placed upon his heart. He then returned to his home. He could never understand why God would send him to preach to an empty shanty.

Many years later in England, as he walked across the London bridge, a man grasped his arm. "I found you at last," the man said. "I think you are mistaken," said Mr. Grellat. "No. Didn't you preach in an empty shanty in the woods of America years ago?" "Yes," Mr. Grellat admitted, "but no one was there."

"I was the foreman in charge of the loggers," the stranger explained. "We had moved to a new location before I realized I'd left one of my tools behind. I returned to get it and heard a voice in one of the shanties; I peered through a crack between the logs and saw you. You never saw me, but I listened to the rest of the sermon. God touched my heart, and I became so convicted of my sin that after some time I purchased a Bible, repented of my sins, and became a Christian. Then I began to win my men to Christ. Your sermon has led at least a thousand people to Christ, and three of them have already become missionaries!"

WESLEY L. DUEWEL, *MEASURE YOUR LIFE*

Patience

Throughout life, one of the hardest words to hear is wait. Sometimes we may anxiously wonder, "Where is God when I need Him?" And yet we are reminded in Scripture, "Blessed are all those who wait for him to help them" (Isaiah 30:18 LB). Patience is developed through faithful waiting. God has a design in even the most difficult situations that will enable our character to become stronger. As we learn patience, we also learn to trust that God has our best interests in mind. He cannot abandon us, and He will always rescue us at just the right time.

Nature Inspires Patience

Throughout life, patience is the virtue many people find most difficult to attain and practice. The seasonal workings of nature can provide the perfect inspiration.

Patience. That was the virtue grandma admonished me to practice as I waited for the strawberries to ripen. It seemed the closer I watched the plants, the greener the tiny berries became! "Be patient," she said. "Them berries are on a schedule all their own, and you trampin' about in the patch won't hurry them up one bit." But patience was a hard lesson for me to learn. I wanted my marigold seeds to sprout and bloom within the week. I wanted Candy,  my white-faced cow, to calf as soon as the neighbors had loaded up their bull and pulled out of our drive. But over the years, farming became a good teacher of patience. I learned that each season had its own charm as well as its own chores. I learned to savor anticipation almost as much as realization. I tried hard to heed the advice of poet Ralph Waldo Emerson: "Adopt the pace of nature: her secret is patience."

As I grew older, I became impatient to get my driver's license, to begin dating, to graduate from high school, to enroll in college. During those adolescent years, Grandma would often open her Bible and read James 5:7–8 to me: "Be patient.... See how the farmer waits for the land to yield its valuable crop and how patient he is for the fall and spring rains. You too, be patient and stand firm." I would take a deep breath and promise to try.

MARY LOU CARNEY, *SPIRITUAL HARVEST*

Teach Me to Wait Patiently

Waiting,
endless waiting.
Why does it seem impossible
to wait patiently
and
graciously—
    for the overdue phone call
    or the long-expected letter...
    for delayed company to arrive
    or a sick one to get better?

Is there a special ingredient
to fill the waiting time
and ease the heavy burdens
that weigh upon my mind?

Could waiting possibly achieve a
    work
which nothing else can do?
God, teach me to
wait patiently
and put full trust
in You.

The Riches of Patience

The best way to deal with the pressures of everyday life is to patiently rely on God.

Life is not easy to any of us. No branch escapes the pruning-knife; no jewel the wheel; no child the rod. People tyrannize over and vex us almost beyond endurance. Circumstances strain us till the chords of our hearts threaten to snap. Our nervous system is overtaxed by the run and competition of our times. Indeed, we have need of patience! ...

And we cannot live such a life till we have learnt to avail ourselves of the riches of the indwelling Christ. The beloved Apostle speaks of being a partaker of the patience which is in Jesus (Rev. 1:9). So may we be. That calm, unmurmuring, unreviling patience, which made the Lamb of God dumb before His shearers, is ours.

F. B. Meyer, *The Secret of Guidance*

Don't be impatient. Wait for the Lord, and he will come and save you! Be brave, stouthearted and courageous. Yes, wait and he will help you.

Psalm 27:14 LB

It is better to be patient than powerful; it is better to have self-control than to conquer a city.

PROVERBS 16:32 NLT

Overwhelmed?

Are insurmountable problems about to do you in? Are you nearly overwhelmed with difficulties, emergencies, and trials of all kinds?

These may be divinely appointed instruments for the Holy Spirit to use in your life. It could take days or even weeks, but if you are patient and willing to find out how God plans to use your current struggles, they can become an avenue for spiritual growth. Problems can turn into possibilities. Tribulations can become blessings that God could get to you in no other way. Bring all your problems to the Lord. Hold them up to Him in prayer. Sit quietly, and wait for him to work. Your restless fretting accomplishes nothing. Rest! Wait! Pray! Do nothing that you are not thoroughly convinced in your spirit He is leading you to do. Give God a chance to work. The insurmountable problems that you face today will become God's opportunity to reveal His love and grace to you as you have never known before.

Patience Develops Character

We can rejoice, too, when we run into problems and trials for we know that they are good for us — they help us learn to be patient. And patience develops strength of character in us and helps us trust God more each time we use it until finally our hope and faith are strong and steady.

ROMANS 5:3–4 LB

Learning to Live Patiently

Rejoice when I run into problems?
Know trials are good for me?
Things like that aren't easy —
Learning to live patiently.

Growing in grace is a process.
Developing character hurts.
Becoming more Christ-like in all
        things
Is an everyday process called work.

But if I have faith it is possible.
Faith knowing God loves and
        cares —
That all of my burdens and trials
He also feels and shares.

Use Your Trials

The trials that come into our lives are the opportunities through which we learn patience.

Use your trials. What is the purpose of the testing? God makes our trials the instrument of blessing. Too often our trials work impatience, but God will give grace that His real purpose may be accomplished. Patience is more necessary than anything else in our faith life. We forget that time is nothing with God, for with Him a thousand years is as one day, and one day as a thousand years. Christ's purpose in our lives is that we shall be perfect and entire, wanting nothing.

HENRIETTA C. MEARS, *WHAT THE BIBLE IS ALL ABOUT*

The Patience of Faith

We may need to endure hard times, but we can trust that whatever happens is part of God's plan.

Patience is more than endurance. A saint's life is in the hands of God like a bow and arrow in the hands of an archer. God is aiming at something the saint cannot see, and He stretches and strains, and every now and again the saint says—"I cannot stand any more." God does not heed, He goes on stretching till His purpose is in sight, then He lets fly. Trust yourself in God's hands. For what have you need of patience just now? Maintain your relationship to Jesus Christ by the patience of faith. "Though He slay me, yet will I wait for Him."

OSWALD CHAMBERS, *MY UTMOST FOR HIS HIGHEST*

Patience I Don't Easily Learn

God, I know you're not in a
    hurry—
Your plans for me are on time.
You need no schedule or reminders
For I'm always on your mind.

I know you have drawn the mosaic
And you're fitting each tile in place.
As I continue to follow your plan,
Help me not to hurry or race.

Waiting is so often difficult,
And patience I don't easily learn.
But to have my life more Christ-
    like
Is for what I seek and yearn.

So as my life's pattern continues
And the next part begins to unfold,
It's you I'm trusting and praising,
It's your hand I cling to and hold.

I Must Be Patient

"On the day I called, you answered me, you increased my strength of soul" (Psalm 138:3 NRSV).

God hears my cries for help, and
He answers every prayer.
I only need be patient—
He supplies the "how" and
    "where."

Sometimes it may be immediate
In a tangible way I'll know;
While other times I wait assured
That He is strengthening my soul:

His grace is all-sufficient
To meet my heart-felt need.
As I lean upon His promises,
Walking in faith, He'll lead.

*A patient man has great understanding,
but a quick-tempered man displays folly.*

PROVERBS 14:29 NIV

Learning to Wait Patiently

We often need to patiently endure time and experience in order to be fully prepared for whatever it is God has planned for our lives. This is illustrated in the Bible by the wilderness experience of Moses, who spent 80 years in preparation for the commission God gave him.

It had taken years, but now Moses had slowed down enough from the maddening pace of life to have time to stop and listen.

"I will go over and see this strange sight—why the bush does not burn up," he mused.

From that moment, all his life was altered. The door, which had been closed so long it resembled the wall, suddenly opened. For as he approached the bush, a voice spoke, calling him by name: "Moses, Moses!"

That voice still speaks to wilderness wanderers. Though the day may seem to be a day like every other day, and the bush like all bushes, things are not always as they seem. Elizabeth Barrett Browning captured the concept:

> Earth's crammed with heaven,
> And every common bush afire
>   with God;
> But only he who sees takes off
>   his shoes. . . .

The tragedy of our wilderness experience is not that we have to go through grief and suffering, but that we often miss the blessings

from burning bushes—the things through which God speaks. Through a letter from a friend, the words of a book, a long-forgotten song, the voice of a teacher, the beauty of a holy life, the innocence of a child, God still calls us by name and makes His eternal purpose known....

Learning to wait patiently, learning to do today what your hand finds to do, learning to hear the call of God when it comes, and to respond—that is what the wilderness is all about. Once a man submits his life to God's control, he voluntarily surrenders the right to determine or the power to vary the consequences of that decision. From that moment on, no situation can ever come into the life of the believer which has not first passed through the hands of God and thus had redeeming quality....

To all those wandering in the wilderness, let it be said: bushes still catch on fire and God still calls men by their names. But the call comes only to those who are busy with the smaller tasks already assigned.

JAMIE BUCKINGHAM, *A WAY THROUGH THE WILDERNESS*

To Be Patient

It is difficult to be patient, especially when we are waiting for something we cannot see—like salvation.

For in hope we were saved. Now hope that is seen is not hope. For who hopes for what is seen? But if we hope for what we do not see, we wait for it with patience.

ROMANS 8:24–25 NRSV

Be glad for all God is planning for you. Be patient in trouble, and always be prayerful.

ROMANS 12:12 NLT

Pray with Patience

"And we know that all things work together for good to them that love God, to them who are called according to his purpose" (Romans 8:28 KJV).

Should you, however, not at once obtain answers to your prayers, be not discouraged; but continue patiently, believingly, perseveringly to wait upon God: and as assuredly as that which you ask would be for your real good, and therefore for the honor of the Lord; and as assuredly as you ask it solely on the ground of the worthiness of the Lord Jesus, so assuredly you will at last obtain the blessing. I myself have had to wait upon God concerning certain matters for years, before I obtained answers to my prayers; but at last they came.

GEORGE MULLER

But they that wait upon the Lord shall renew their strength; they shall mount up with wings as eagles; they shall run, and not be weary; and they shall walk, and not faint.

ISAIAH 40:31 KJV

If you've tried and have not won,
Never stop for crying;
All that's great and good is done
Just by patient trying.

PHOEBE CARY

Forty Days and Nights

One of the all-time favorite Bible stories is that of the Great Flood. Besides being a wonderful story, it also provides valuable lessons about patience and faith.

I can see Noah and his three sons felling the huge cypress trees, hacking off the bark and hewing the trunks into water-worthy planks, while their wicked peers jeered and shouted insults. For years they worked on that boat, in a spot so far inland that a scarcity of water seemed a more impending threat than a profusion of rain. As he hammered and planed and sawed, Noah preached. His topic was always the same: repentance. But his neighbors were

more interested in sensual pleasures, in greed and gluttony, in idolatry and innocent bloodshed.

Then the rains began. Drops the size of grapes plopped onto the dust around the ark. Their patter turned to pounding, and inside the ark Noah and his family knew it was true. God was destroying the world. Only they and the animals on board would survive.

For the next year, Noah and the others on the ark lived in a world of bobbing isolation. At first they heard the cries of now-penitent people, the terrified screams of jackals and wolves. But soon these sounds were silenced by the slosh of waves, by the reality of water rising higher than the mountains.

What patience Noah had! During those long years of labor, during those long months of confinement, he did not rant or rail. He waited. He did not pace in panic. He waited. And one morning, as sunlight streamed through the solitary window and patterned the worn deck, Noah knew it was time. He released a dove. She came back by nightfall, unable to find a resting place. For almost a month he sent forth this bird. Although he longed for respite from his watery

world—longed to see the rough beauty of tree bark and to feel the earth beneath his feet—Noah knew that this was no time to be impulsive. It was no time to lead the remnants of creation into an unsure situation. Finally, the dove did not return. Then Noah was certain that the ground was indeed dry, that the fury of God's judgment had passed.

The huge door of the ark creaked open. Foxes and camels blinked into the brightness. Birds fluttered their folded wings and fumbled into flight. Lions tossed their manes as memories stirred of star-filled nights spent stalking prey.

What did Noah do? Rush headlong out into this new world? Boast at having beaten the odds? Organize committees to establish a new community? Hardly! "Then Noah built an altar to the Lord and, taking some of all the clean animals and clean birds, he sacrificed burnt offerings on it" (Genesis 8:20). Even in this time of great jubilation, of enormous challenge, Noah's priorities and patience were intact. He paused to offer thanks. And God, pleased with Noah, promised never again to destroy all living creatures.

"As long as the earth
    endures,
seedtime and harvest,
cold and heat,
summer and winter,
day and night
will never cease."
Genesis 8:22

What did Noah do then? He planted a vineyard, and, sure of God's promise, settled down to watch it grow. To *patiently* watch it grow.

MARY LOU CARNEY, SPIRITUAL HARVEST

Maturity: facing each new day with patience, calmness, and confidence that God is in control.

Let Patience Have Her Perfect Work

Any great work of art takes time to be perfected in the hands of the master artist.

Let patience have her perfect work. Statue under the chisel of the sculptor, stand steady to the blows of his mallet. Clay on the wheel, let the fingers of the divine potter model you at their will. Obey the Father's lightest word: hear the Brother who knows you and died for you.

GEORGE MACDONALD, *RIGHTEOUSNESS*

Brothers and sisters, we urge you to warn those who are lazy. Encourage those who are timid. Take tender care of those who are weak. Be patient with everyone.

1 THESSALONIANS 5:15 NLT

Honesty

We all prefer to deal with honest people — people we can trust — people who will not lie or try to deceive us. A noble goal for one's life is to pursue honesty — honesty with others, with ourselves, and with God. Yet it is not natural to tell the truth. Honesty can seem to leave us open to attack — to tear down the walls of protection we would rather erect in our lives. Scripture tells us, "The truth shall make you free." Although it might be hard to be honest, if we do it with loving intentions, the burden that dishonesty brings will be lifted.

The Depths of Honesty

Honesty is more than just not telling lies. It begins inside us with our motives and moves outward to how we deal with people.

Honesty is more complex than simply not stealing money or not telling a bold lie. Honesty involves our deepest motives and encompasses every area of private and public life. It includes truth in every sense, and integrity in the inner person. Honesty demands putting aside lying, cheating, slander, and deceit—and, at times, even silence.

JERRY WHITE, *HONESTY, MORALITY & CONSCIENCE*

Qualities of an Honest Man

What we do when a lie is exposed determines our level of honesty. An honest person sincerely desires to face up to their lies and get back to the truth.

An honest man is not a man who never lies. There is no such man. When an honest man is caught in a lie or discovers he has lied, he is quick to admit it. He then speaks the truth. He's not afraid to say, "Please forgive me for not being honest." He does not defend a lie. Unlike a dishonest man, he does not make plans to lie or use lies to cover other falsehoods. He regularly scrutinizes his life to see if he has lied or is living a lie in any area. Honesty with God, his fellow man, and himself is the honest man's goal and his heart's desire.

Hard are the ways of truth, and rough to walk. JOHN MILTON, PARADISE REGAINED

The High Cost of Dishonesty

It's sometimes hard to face others with the truth and deal with the consequences. But if we keep the truth concealed, we will always pay the price.

When Mrs. Loisel took back the jewels to Mrs. Forestier, the latter said to her in a frigid tone:
"You should have returned them sooner, for I might have needed them."

She did open the jewel-box as her friend feared she would. If she should perceive substitution, what would she think? What would she say? Would she take her for a robber?

Mrs. Loisel now knew the horrible life of necessity. She did her part, however, completely, heroically. It was necessary to pay this frightful debt. She would pay it. They sent away the maid; they changed their lodgings; they rented some rooms under a mansard roof.

She learned the heavy cares of a household, the odious work of a kitchen. She washed the dishes, using her rosy nails upon the greasy pots and the bottoms of the stewpans. She washed the soiled linen, the chemises and dishcloths, which she hung on the line to dry; she took down the refuse to the street each morning and brought up the water, stopping at each landing to breathe. And, clothed like a woman of the people, she went to the grocer's, the butcher's, and the fruiterer's, with her basket on her arm, shopping, haggling, defending to the last sou her miserable money.

Every month it was necessary to renew some notes, thus obtaining time, and to pay others.

The husband worked evenings, putting the books of some merchants in order, and nights he often did copying at five sous a page.

And this lasted for ten years.

At the end of ten years, they had restored all, all, with interest of the usurer, and accumulated interest besides.

Mrs. Loisel seemed old now. She had become a strong, hard woman of the poor household. Her hair badly dressed, her skirts awry, her hands red, she spoke in a loud tone, and washed the floors, using large pails of water. But sometimes, when her husband was at the office, she would seat herself before the window and think of that evening party of former times, of that ball where she was so beautiful and so flattered.

How would it have been if she had not lost that necklace? Who knows? Who knows? How singular is life, and how full of changes! How small a thing will ruin or save one!

One Sunday, as she was taking a walk in the Champs-Elysees to rid herself of the cares of the week, she suddenly perceived a woman walking with a child. It was Mrs. Forestier, still young, still pretty, still attractive. Mrs. Loisel was affected. Should she speak to her? Yes, certainly. And now that she had paid, she would tell her all. Why not?

She approached her. "Good morning, Jeanne."

Her friend did not recognize her and was astonished to be so familiarly addressed by this common personage. She stammered:

"But, Madame—I do not know—You must be mistaken—"

"No, I am Matilda Loisel."

Her friend uttered a cry of astonishment: "Oh! my poor Matilda! How you have changed—"

"Yes, I have had some hard days since I saw you; and some miserable ones—and all because of you—"

"Because of me? How is that?"

"You recall the diamond necklace that you loaned me to wear to the Commissioner's ball?"

"Yes, very well."

"Well, I lost it."

"How is that, since you returned it to me?"

"I returned another to you exactly like it. And it has taken us ten years to pay for it. You can understand that it was not easy for us who have nothing. But it is finished and I am decently content."

Madame Forestier stopped short. She said:

"You say that you bought a diamond necklace to replace mine?"

"Yes. You did not perceive it then? They were just alike?"

And she smiled with a proud simple joy. Madame Forestier was touched and took both her hands as she replied:

"Oh! my poor Matilda! Mine were false. They were not worth over five hundred francs!"

GUY DE MAUPASSANT, "THE DIAMOND NECKLACE"

God's View of Lies

*Honesty is obviously a very impor-
tant trait in God's eyes. He detests
lying so much that it is mentioned
twice on this list of things he hates.*

There are six things the Lord
hates, seven that are
detestable to him;
haughty eyes,
a lying tongue,
hands that shed innocent blood,
a heart that devises wicked
schemes,
feet that are quick to rush into evil,
a false witness who pours out lies
and a man who stirs up dissension
among brothers.

PROVERBS 6:16–19 NIV

*Dishonesty builds
a wall between two
people. Only the
hammer of truth can
break the wall down.*

*No legacy is
so rich as honesty.*

WILLIAM SHAKESPEARE,
ALL'S WELL THAT ENDS WELL

Dishonesty Under Pressure

We are all capable of dishonesty. Even Jesus' close friend Peter lied when he was under pressure and his life seemed in danger. Later, though, he traveled around boldly proclaiming the truth.

The soldiers lit a fire in the courtyard and sat around it for warmth, and Peter joined them there.

A servant girl noticed him in the firelight and began staring at him. Finally she spoke: "This man was with Jesus!"

Peter denied it. "Woman," he said, "I don't even know the man!"

After a while someone else looked at him and said, "You must be one of them!"

"No sir, I am not!" Peter replied.

About an hour later someone else flatly stated, "I know this fellow is one of Jesus' disciples, for both are from Galilee."

But Peter said, "Man, I don't know what you are talking about." And as he said the words, a rooster crowed.

At that moment Jesus turned and looked at Peter. Then Peter remembered what he had said—"Before the rooster crows tomorrow morning, you will deny me three times." And Peter walked out of the courtyard, crying bitterly.

LUKE 22:55–62 LB

Honesty Versus Keeping the Peace

Being honest with our feelings is difficult, but dishonesty builds walls in relationships. When we are honest with others about how we feel, we are drawn closer together.

Years ago I saw a television show where a camera was hidden in a restaurant. An actor entered, sat next to a man eating at the counter, and without saying a word, grabbed some French fries off the man's plate. This scenario was repeated numerous times, and nine times out of ten the victims never said a word. You knew they were doing a slow burn inside; they clenched their fists and glared at the thief in disbelief. But they never said a word.

When people submerge their true feelings in order to preserve harmony, they undermine the integrity of a relationship. They buy peace on the surface, but underneath there are hurt feelings, troubling questions, and hidden hostilities just waiting to erupt. It's a costly price to pay for a cheap peace, and it inevitably leads to inauthentic relationships.

BILL HYBELS, *HONEST TO GOD?*

Part of Love Is Honesty

It's not always easy to tell the truth when another person asks us a question. Many times we know they don't really want to hear the truth. Yet, if we want love to grow, honesty is a fertile soil.

If I really love you, don't I have to be honest with you? When you ask me, "Was it me? Or was it them?" when caught in a conflict, I can't always take your side, even though it seems like the loving thing to do. But is it really loving, or just easiest? If I truly love you, I will stop being afraid to say, "My friend, sometimes you are wrong." I don't want to listen to the lie anymore—the one that says, "If you love and accept me, you will never confront me." I want what's best for you, and sometimes that best will come when I am honest about the worst I see in you. The

test of true love comes when I speak the truth in love—when I risk being honest about your dark side. If you walk away, then I know that although I loved you enough to be honest, you did not love me enough to let me be.

Telling the Truth About Pain

Sometimes we put up a false front, even with our closest friends and loved ones. We think, "What would happen if they knew what's really going on with me?" When we stop hiding behind a "happy face," we open the door to true intimacy.

Too often we lie
when people ask,
"How are you?"
We say, "I'm fine."
We smile and put
on our happy face.

Why can't we be honest,
at least with loved ones,
and say, "I hurt"?
Why can't we cry honest
        tears
and let a friend
comfort us for a
        moment—
embrace us
with loving arms,
as we take off
the mask we wear
to hide the pain?

Lying lips are an abomination to the Lord, But those who deal truthfully are His delight.

PROVERBS 12:22 NKJV

Telling Ourselves the Truth

Though we may feel noble when we brutally tell people the truth about their faults, we need to be honest about our own faults first. After we've done that, our honesty becomes gentler.

"Do not judge lest you be judged yourselves.

"For in the way you judge, you will be judged; and by your standard of measure, it shall be measured to you.

"And why do you look at the speck in your brother's eye, but do not notice the log that is in your own eye?

"Or how can you say to your brother, 'Let me take the speck out of your eye,' and behold, the log is in your own eye?

"You hypocrite, first take the log out of your own eye, and then you will see clearly enough to take the speck out of your brother's eye."

Matthew 7:1–5 NASB

Plunging into the Depths of Honesty

The truth can be difficult to face, but if we are always desiring to seek and face the truth, our lives will be much richer. Being willing to dig deeper for truth is a sign of godliness.

Our work is not only to be done thoroughly, but it is to be done honestly. A man is not only to be honorable in his academic relations, but he must be honest with himself and in his attitude toward the truth. Students are not entitled to dodge difficulties, they must go down to the foundation principles. Perhaps the truths which are dear to us go down even deeper than we think, and we will get more out of them if we dig down for the nuggets than we will if we only pick up those that are on the surface. Other theories may perhaps be found to have false bases; if so, we ought to know it. It is well to take our soundings in every direction to see if there is deep water; if there are shoals we ought to find out where they are. Therefore, when we come to difficulties, let us not jump lightly over them, but let us be honest as seekers after truth.

HENRY DRUMMOND,
THE GREATEST THING IN THE WORLD

Truth and Consequences

Be brave, my soul—
Let go of lies.
Stop deceiving yourself.
Have courage
to embrace the truth
and all its consequences.

An honest man's the noblest work of God.

ALEXANDER POPE, "AN ESSAY ON MAN"

Move On to Telling the Truth

Don't lie to one another. You're done with that old life. It's like a filthy set of ill-fitting clothes you've stripped off and put in the fire. Now you're dressed in a new wardrobe.

COLOSSIANS 3:9–10 THE MESSAGE

Honesty is the best policy.

MIGUEL DE CERVANTES,
DON QUIXOTE

Honesty as a Student

Many people defend lying, because "everyone is doing it." To go along with the lies of others is to be dishonest ourselves. It takes courage to expose dishonesty.

The chatter in the room dwindled to a few nervous comments and jokes as the professor began passing out the exams. Several students hastily reviewed their notes. Others sat nervously tapping their pencils on the desks. The normal pre-exam tension filled the air....

The professor gave a few brief words of explanation and walked out of the room, leaving two student proctors to monitor the exam and answer questions. There was a rustle of relief as soon as he left. Crib sheets emerged, books opened, and dozens of students began cheating blatantly.

One student, however, saw the obvious cheating and became inwardly agitated. A former cadet at the United States Air Force Academy, he was now working on a special assignment to complete his master's degree. He had been trained for four years under an honor code at the academy.

Finally, he stood up and announced to the class, "What you people are doing is wrong! It is cheating! I can't stand for it and I plan to report this ...!"

He sat down as abruptly as he had stood. The class was speechless. Then a new wave of nervousness swept across the room.

After the exam several students congratulated the student for his courage. Cheating bothered them too, they said, but it was so common they had felt unable to do anything.

The student reported the cheating, and the exams were discarded and a new test was administered. What was accomplished by his action? It didn't stop all the cheating, but a clear standard of right was established in the class. Others were given courage to act on their convictions in the future, and the student himself had a strengthened sense of integrity and the peace of a clear conscience.

JERRY WHITE, *HONESTY, MORALITY &*
CONSCIENCE

Solomon's Wisdom About Honesty

Lies will get any man into trouble, but honesty is its own defense (Proverbs 12:13 LB).

Telling the truth gives a man great satisfaction (Proverbs 12:14 LB).

A good man is known by his truthfulness; a false man by deceit and lies (Proverbs 12:17 LB).

Truth stands the test of time; lies are soon exposed (Proverbs 12:19 LB).

Honorable Title

I hope I shall always possess firmness and virtue enough to maintain what I consider the most enviable of all titles, the character of an "Honest Man."

GEORGE WASHINGTON

We Need God's Help to Be Honest

We can never be completely
     honest on our own.
It is human nature to lie.
That's why when a witness
who takes the stand in a court of
     law is asked,
"Do you solemnly swear
to tell the truth, the whole truth,
and nothing but the truth,"
the phrase is added,
"so help
me God."

Honesty Means We Stop Pretending

*Honest people are real, especially
before God. When we pretend that
everything is fine or that we are
self-sufficient, the one that ends up
getting hurt is us. Pretending only
weakens us and our relationships.*

If we could stop pretending to be
     strong
and start being honest with
     ourselves and God,
crying out, "God, please help!
I am poor and needy,"
He would hurry to help us
and be the strength of our lives.

*And you will
know the truth, and
the truth will set you
free.*

JOHN 8:32 LB

Forgiveness

*F*orgiveness is the central virtue in God's treasure chest—God's forgiveness of us, and our forgiveness of others, God, and ourselves. We've all stood in the midst of the Sunday congregation praying, "Forgive us our sins as we forgive those who sin against us." At times we find that forgiveness comes very easily, even for grievous and painful hurts. But many times, we seem powerless to forgive, no matter how hard we try. This is when God's forgiving grace has the opportunity to touch and change us and then be extended to others through our example.

Forgiveness

Snow
that fell
so softly in the night
changed earth's soot to white
in glistening loveliness.

Forgiveness
like soft snow
gently covers the soil
and lo
ugliness is beauty!

LUCILLE GARDNER

Preparing to Forgive

*Our emotional release of the past and its pain will, in large measure,
determine our ability to move on into constructive future relationships.*

Forgiveness is letting what was, be gone; what will be, come; what is
now, be.

In forgiving, I finish my demands on past predicaments, problems,
failures and say good-by to them with finality. I cancel my predictions,
suspicions, premonitions of failure and welcome the next moment with
openness to discover what will be. I make a new transaction of affirming
integrity between us now. . . .

Forgiveness is willingly accepting the other on the basis of our loving and leveling, of our caring and confronting, agreeing to be genuine
with each other here, now and in the future.

Forgiveness is being willing to let it be with the best that we can
achieve now and move on into the future without repressing my own
spontaneous response to you or seeking to restrict yours.

DAVID AUGSBURGER, *CARING ENOUGH TO FORGIVE*

The Biblical Theme of Forgiveness

Because none of us will ever be able to live a perfect life, we need to be understanding and practice forgiveness in our daily lives.

Forgiveness is a theme that runs throughout the pages of the Bible. When we confess our sins to Jesus Christ, we are promised that he will forgive (1 John 1:9). Then, in the Lord's prayer, we are instructed to forgive others just as Christ forgave us (Matthew 6:12).

To forgive is to pardon completely and to forget the offense forever, without holding a grudge and without maintaining an attitude of condescending superiority because of what we have done.

There are times when every human being loses control. We explode in anger, say things that should not have been said, gossip, harbor jealousy or envy...or otherwise give in to subtle temptations. Sometimes we admit these tendencies, at least to ourselves, and recognize the presence of guilt because of our thoughts or actions. At other times we pretend to "have it all together" and walk about like the Pharisees of old claiming to be something that we are not....

Whenever we lose control or slip into sin we can confess directly to God and know for certain that he will forgive without requiring that we do anything to atone for our wrongdoing.

At times, however, there can be value in confessing not only to God but to our fellow human beings. One way to care for others is to confess to one another, pray for one another,  forgive one another, and accept each other with all of our human imperfections (James 5:16; Ephesians 4:32; Romans 15:7). Since God is clearly willing to forgive, we have a responsibility to do the same.

GARY R. COLLINS, *THE JOY OF CARING*

Times for Forgiveness

It is fine to read about how God asks us to forgive others, but it is much better to actually forgive others. And we would do well to forgive others again and again.

When Tom worked with a group of Girl Scouts on their God and Family Award, they talked about how often the girls squabbled with friends and how hard it was to make up. Tom told them about the conversation between Jesus and Peter when Peter asked about the number of times they need to forgive.

The girls gazed at Tom as he asked them to add 70 plus 7; "*77!*" one child replied.

"So that's how often we are to forgive other people," Tom explained. Silence. The girls looked at each other, appalled. Then one girl spoke up, "That's too hard. I think I'll just ignore that rule."

Tom then explained how most everyone has at least some rules they would rather ignore. Although Jesus gives everyone practical advice about living together, his words have little meaning until they are put into practice. Anyone can hear his words; it takes loving discipline to obey his commandments.

Forgive us, Lord, our sins, for failing to live
up to your standards of goodness and justice.
We confess our shortcomings. Make us willing to change, and help us become persons of
godly character. Amen.

Redemption

*God knows that as hard as we may try, there are times when we will
make human mistakes. Even so, if we trust in Him and ask His forgiveness, He will bless us with mercy and peace.*

The Lord hath spoken peace to
    my soul,
He hath blessed me abundantly,
Hath pardoned my sins;
He hath shown me great mercy
    and saved me by his love.
I will sing of his goodness and
    mercy while I live,
And ever, forever will praise his
    holy name.
O how sweet to trust in God,
And to know your sins forgiven,
To believe his precious word,
And be guided by his love.
Therefore goodness and mercy,
Shall follow me all the days of
    my life.
Amen.

C. E. LESLIE, *LESLIE'S CROWN OF SONG*

Mercy, Forgiveness, and Pardon

These three words, as taught from an 1896 school textbook, appear to be similar on the surface, yet they are very different when we look closely at the definitions.

Mercy is the exercise of less severity than one deserves, or in a more extended sense, the granting of *kindness* or *favor* beyond what one may rightly claim. *Grace* is *favor, kindness,* or *blessing* shown to the undeserving; *forgiveness, mercy* and *pardon* are exercised toward the ill-deserving. *Pardon* remits the outward penalty which the offender deserves; *forgiveness* dismisses resentment or displeasure from the heart of the one offended; *mercy* seeks the highest possible good of the offender. . . .

To *pardon* is to let pass, as a fault or sin, without resentment, blame, or punishment. *Forgive* has reference to feelings, *pardon* to consequences; hence, the executive may *pardon,* but has nothing to do officially with *forgiving.* Personal injury may be *forgiven* by the person wronged; thus, God at once *forgives* and *pardons*; the *pardoned* sinner is exempt from punishment; the *forgiven* sinner is restored to the divine favor. To *pardon* is the act of a superior, implying the right to punish; to *forgive* is the privilege of the humblest person who has been wronged or offended.

JAMES C. FERNALD, *ENGLISH SYNONYMS AND ANTONYMS*

Feelings or Fact?

The story is told that someone asked Martin Luther if he "felt" that he had been forgiven. His reply:

> "No, but I'm as sure
> As there's a God in Heaven.
> For feelings come, and feelings go,
> And feelings are deceiving.
> My warrant is the Word of God,
> Naught else is worth believing."

And thus it has remained down through the ages. Many times we may come to the place where it is difficult to "feel" forgiven. That is where faith comes in. And the very basis of the Christian faith is a belief in a God that cannot lie. "I acknowledged my sin unto thee, and mine iniquity have I not hid. I said, I will confess my transgressions unto the Lord; and thou forgavest the iniquity of my sin" (Psalm 32:5 KJV).

Forgiveness is the soil in which God nurtures our emotional healing and our ability to love once again.

JOHN NIEDER AND THOMAS M.
THOMPSON,
FORGIVE & LOVE AGAIN

Jesus Teaches Forgiveness

This familiar Bible story clearly illustrates that when we are shown mercy, we must pass that gift on to others.

Then Peter came and said to him, "Lord, if another member of the church sins against me, how often should I forgive? As many as seven times?" Jesus said to him, "Not seven times, but, I tell you, seventy-seven times.

"For this reason the kingdom of heaven may be compared to a king who wished to settle accounts with his slaves. When he began the reckoning, one who owed him ten thousand talents was brought to him; and, as he could not pay, his lord ordered him to be sold, together with his wife and children and all his posses- sions, and pay- ment to be made. So the slave fell on his knees before him, saying, 'Have patience with me, and I will pay you everything.' And out of pity for him, the lord of that

slave released him and forgave him the debt. But that same slave, as he went out, came upon one of his fellow slaves who owed him a hun- dred denarii, and seizing him by the throat, he said. 'Pay what you owe.' Then his fellow slave fell down and pleaded him, 'Have patience with me, and I will pay you.' But he refused; then he went and threw him into prison until he would pay the debt. When his fellow slaves saw what had happened, they were greatly distressed, and they went and reported to their lord all that had taken place. Then his lord summoned him and said to him, 'You wicked slave! I forgave you all that debt because you pleaded with me. Should you not have had mercy on your fellow slave, as I had mercy on you?' And in anger his lord handed him over to be tortured until he would pay his entire debt. So my heavenly Father will also do to every one of you, if you do not for- give your brother and sister from your heart."

MATTHEW 18:21–35
NRSV

Like God

We should remember to forgive just as
God remembers to forgive us.

Dear Lord and Father of mankind
Forgive our foolish ways;
Reclothe us in our rightful mind,
In purer lives Thy service find,
In deeper reverence, praise.

JOHN GREENLEAF WHITTIER, *THE BREWING OF SOMA*

Beware of Witholding Forgiveness

When we receive God's forgiveness, we should pass it freely on to others. Our example is Christ, who was willing to forgive even those who crucified him.

Our sins are forgiven by God's mercy alone. We can't earn forgiveness by forgiving others. But when we withhold forgiveness from others after having received it ourselves, it shows we don't understand or appreciate God's mercy toward us.

LIFE APPLICATION BIBLE NOTES (JAMES 2:13 LB)

You will be judged on whether or not you are doing what Christ wants you to. So watch what you do and what you think; for there will be no mercy to those who have shown no mercy. But if you have been merciful, then God's mercy toward you will win out over his judgment against you.

JAMES 2:12–13 LB

Blessed Are Those Who Forgive and Are Forgiven

God forgives us our sins. Should we be like God and forgive others' transgressions?

Blessed is he whose transgression is forgiven, whose sin is covered. Blessed is the man unto whom the Lord imputeth not iniquity, and in whose spirit there is no guile.

When I kept silence, my bones waxed old through my roaring all the day long.

For day and night thy hand was heavy upon me: my moisture is turned into the drought of summer. Selah.

I acknowledged my sin unto thee, and mine iniquity have I not hid. I said, I will confess my transgressions unto the Lord; and thou forgavest the iniquity of my sin. Selah.

For this shall every one that is godly pray unto thee in a time when thou mayest be found: surely in the floods of great waters they shall not come nigh unto him.

Thou art my hiding place; thou shalt preserve me from trouble; thou shalt compass me about with songs of deliverance. Selah.

I will instruct thee and teach thee in the way which thou shalt go: I will guide thee with mine eye.

Be ye not as the horse, or as the mule, which have no understanding: whose mouth must be held in with bit and bridle, lest they come near unto thee.

Many sorrows shall be to the wicked: but he that trusteth in the Lord, mercy shall compass him about.

Be glad in the Lord, and rejoice, ye righteous: and shout for joy, all ye that are upright in heart.

PSALM 32 KJV

Forgiveness Comes from God

Even if we find it hard to forgive and love, God's mercy can flow through us to others.

Because of their work hiding Jewish refugees, Corrie and Betsy ten Boom spent years in Ravensbrük, a Nazi concentration camp. Eventually, Betsy died there. After her release from the camp, Corrie ten Boom traveled around the world, preaching a message of God's forgiveness. The strength of her belief was tested, though, when she met one of her former SS jailers at a Munich church where she had just preached.

The sight of the jailer awakened ten Boom's painful memories of the camp. When he came forward to shake her hand, she was stunned to hear him say that Jesus had died for his sins also! Corrie ten Boom was unable to lift her hand to meet his. She couldn't even manage a smile. So she prayed for Jesus to forgive her and for help to forgive the man. She was still unable to respond. When she prayed that she could not forgive him, and she asked only for forgiveness for herself, she felt a current of love shoot down her arm toward the man she had every reason to hate.

But love your enemies, do good, and lend, expecting nothing in return.

LUKE 6:35

Forgiveness — The Precondition of Love

Forgiveness is not dependent on our feelings, but is rather a determination of our will.

Forgiveness is the precondition of love. The "how" of forgiveness is through knowing how to use our will — the rudder of our life. We are responsible for the set of this rudder; once we have willed a course of action, God will be responsible for our feelings if we will hand them over to Him. Otherwise, nothing we can do would change these feelings.

When I put that conclusion along side David du Plessis' statement, "Forgiveness means, 'The other person may be as wrong as wrong can be, but I'll not be the judge,'" I saw that forgiveness is simply the decision of our wills to release a particular person, followed by verbalizing that to God. It can be a simple prayer like, "Lord, I release ____ from my judgment.  Forgive me that I may have bound him and hampered Your work by judging. Now I step out of the way so that Heaven can go into action for _____." Obviously, there is nothing impossible about praying like that.

CATHERINE MARSHALL, SOMETHING MORE

A few well-chosen words of forgiveness are like an antiseptic that cleanses the wound and promotes healing.

Divine Forgiveness

The biblical story of the prodigal son reminds us that God is eager to forgive us, and it prompts us to be ready to forgive others.

To understand divine forgiveness we must turn to the teachings of Jesus. His parable of the prodigal son illustrates it best. The younger of two sons leaves home in reckless, youthful disregard of the father's love. In a distant country he squanders his money with dissolute companions who desert him when his money is gone. Reduced to tending swine — unspeakable depths to a Jew — he begins to compare his hunger and loneliness with the abundance and love he had experienced at home. Suddenly he resolves to return home: "I will arise and go to my father, and I will say to him, 'Father I have sinned . . .'" (Luke 15:11–24).

The father rushes down the road to welcome the returning son. The young man begins his carefully rehearsed speech of repentance, but the father cuts it short with his glad welcome. The son's repentance is obvious; nothing matters to the father but that his son has returned. The father has not waited until now to extend forgiveness. In his mind the son was always forgiven. But he could not be aware of or accept or be healed by that forgiveness until he returned in repentance.

CECIL OSBORNE, *THE ART OF UNDERSTANDING YOURSELF*

An Unlikely Forgiveness

For decades, preachers have retold this story of the late Rev. Mr. Lee, who was a Presbyterian minister in Waterford, New York.

It was midnight. Mr. Lee was still in his study preparing the Sunday morning sermon. Suddenly a strange noise aroused him. He felt the presence of someone else in the room.

"Who is it? What is the matter?" he called, turning around in his desk chair.

He was face-to-face with a grim burglar pointing a gun directly at him. The robber, thinking that all of the occupants were fast asleep, had entered the house through a side window.

"Give me your watch and money," he demanded, "and make no noise, or I will shoot."

"You may put down your gun. I will make no resistance. You are at liberty to take all of the valuables I possess," was Mr. Lee's calm reply. "I will lead you to where my most precious treasures are stored."

They walked down the hall where he opened the door to an adjoining room. He pointed to the bed where his two children lay innocently sleeping. "Those," he said, "are my choicest jewels. Will you take them?"

He proceeded to tell the would-be burglar that, as a minister of the Gospel, he owned very few earthly possessions. What little money he did earn was all devoted to one purpose—to educate these two motherless children.

The burglar was deeply and visibly moved by these remarks. Tears filled his eyes as he said, "Please, sir, forgive me, I didn't know. I am so sorry to have troubled you, and so sorry for the act which I was about to commit."

Mr. Lee's well-chosen words convicted this would-be criminal. Then he invited him to kneel right there and join him in prayer.

God had softened the heart of this burglar, and he consented to pray the sinner's prayer, pouring forth his remorse and penitence.

Mr. Lee was able to assure him of the Scripture, "If we confess our sins, he is faithful and just to forgive us our sins, and to cleanse us from all unrighteousness" (1 John 1:9 KJV). Mr. Lee showed the man to the door with these words, "Go, and sin no more."

Now is the time to forgive this man and help him back on his feet. If all you do is pour on the guilt, you could very well drown him in it. My counsel now is to pour on the love.

2 CORINTHIANS 2:7–8 THE MESSAGE

A Healing Prayer

Only by calling on God for help are we able to truly forgive and forget.

Father, forgiveness can be an arduous process. We can be stubborn and refuse to forgive. But by not forgiving others we are hurting ourselves, too. Please help us to release our resentment so it doesn't consume us. We look to you for guidance. Amen.

The Practice of Forgiveness

Even if we feel we've been wronged by someone, if we soften our hearts and forgive the one who wronged us, the burden of bitterness will be lifted. This change is certain to affect the lives of those around us.

There is nothing more healing in all the world than when one starts to practice forgiveness. It's not always easy to forgive, but it's far more difficult not to. When Jesus was so unjustly treated, how did he react? The answer is he didn't react, he responded. Jesus—the responder—forgave them. Jesus cried as the blood spurted from his heart,

"Father, forgive them, for they know not what they do." Jesus taught that we were to forgive an unlimited number of times (Matthew 18:21, 22). Disciples asked the Lord how many times they should forgive and Jesus said seven times seventy. Then he added that if we don't forgive others, then we can't be forgiven our sins.

Only the offended can forgive.

A wife was left alone evening after evening. Her resentments turned to hate. She started keeping a hate book, actually writing down in a notebook every night her husband was gone from home, and the exact number of minutes. It got so bad he spent only two evenings home in seven weeks, always finding excuses to be away. His wife would constantly badger him about this in the few minutes he would be home.

Then the lady began to respond to God's working in her heart. He showed her what her bitter unforgiving spirit was doing, how in the few minutes her husband was at home, she was driving him further and further away from home and herself. She read the challenge of Christ in her Bible, to be the first to forgive. Her life took a turn for the better when she said with God's help, "I forgive him." Then she had a second great thought. If she was going to forgive him, it meant throwing the hate book away. She took the hate book and threw it in the fire. That was followed by a great idea. The idea was this—"I will make the most out of those moments when he is home, and make it interesting and pleasant."

Within weeks he began spending more time at home and soon afterward he faced up to the way he had been shortchanging his family. Foundations were laid for a new and more satisfying relationship in the home. Forgiveness is what brought the breath of fresh air and newness to this home.

Forgiveness has healed many a broken relationship, and forgiveness has healed many a wounded spirit.

The healing medicine—forgiveness—is yours for the using.

DALE E. GALLOWAY, *DREAM A NEW DREAM*

Perfect Forgiveness

Sometimes it may seem impossible to forgive other people, especially if they are purposely trying to hurt us. But if Jesus could forgive the people who crucified Him, certainly we can forgive those who have hurt us.

When on the fragrant sandal-tree
   The woodman's axe descends,
And she who bloomed so
     beauteously
   Beneath the keen stroke bends,
E'en on the edge that wrought her
     death
Dying she breathed her sweetest
     breath,
As if to token, in her fall,
Peace to her foes, and love to all.

How hardly man this lesson
     learns,
To smile and bless the hand that
     spurns;
To see the blow, to feel the pain,
But render only love again!
This spirit not to earth is given—
One had it, but he came from
     heaven.
Reviled, rejected, and betrayed,
No curse he breathed, no plaint he
     made,
But when in death's deep pain he
     sighed
Prayed for his murderers, and died.

AUTHOR UNKNOWN

*Judge not, and ye shall not be judged:
condemn not, and ye shall not be condemned:
forgive, and ye shall be forgiven.*

LUKE 6:37 KJV

How to Destroy Your Enemies

An elderly woman asked Abe Lincoln, "How can you speak kindly of your enemies when you should rather destroy them?"

"Madam," he said, "do I not destroy them when I make them my friends?"

CARL SANDBURG

Forgive and You'll Be Forgiven

For if you forgive people their trespasses—that is, their reckless and willful sins, leaving them, letting them go and giving up resentment—your heavenly Father will also forgive you.

But if you do not forgive others . . . neither will your Father forgive you your trespasses.

MATTHEW 6:14–15 AMPLIFIED

Forgiveness Is Not a Gamble

Mercy and forgiveness can help a person toward wholeness.

Fred was an active member of his local church. So when he first asked for a loan from another church member—"Just a few dollars to tide me over"—nothing was made of it. One loan led to another, though, until Fred owed money—lots of it—to almost everyone in the church. Fred's compulsive gambling finally became known when his inability to pay back his loans led to one woman's own financial problems.

Fred apologized for his behavior; however, the pattern repeated as Fred's addiction overcame his desire to begin anew. As difficult as it was, the church members continued to forgive Fred, even though they realized that loaning him money was not the best thing to do since it helped him continue his destructive behavior.

Instead, after the repentance and forgiveness scenario had

played out many times, some members gathered with Fred to talk honestly about his gambling compulsion. The woman whose own finances were in jeopardy because of her loans to Fred even said, "I will go with you to support group meetings. I want to try to understand what your addiction is like."

Fred found a group for recovering gamblers where he heard many stories similar to his: persons struggling with addiction who were occasionally overwhelmed by it, acted hurtfully toward others, repented, and asked for forgiveness. Fred became accountable for his actions and paid back the church members soon after. He never gambled again and continues to be involved with the church community.

Love Depends on Forgiveness

Love and forgiveness walk hand in hand. Our relationships with God and others are intertwined in this dynamic.

Love often succumbs to a cold death on the sharp rocks of disappointment. *Love cannot last long or live out its eternal purpose in human relationships without a foundation of forgiveness* — the forgiveness from God for our failure to love with a pure, other-centered heart, and forgiveness when the recipient of our love spurns our gift or uses our soul in an unloving fashion. Unless the fabric of our involvement with others is woven with the threads of forgiveness, love will suffer the corruption of denial, hard-

ness, cynicism, and eventually hatred. . . .

Love is dependent on forgiveness. A formula can almost be structured from this concept. *The extent to which someone truly loves will be positively correlated to the degree the person is stunned and silenced by the wonder that his huge debt has been canceled.* Perhaps another way to say it is that gratitude for forgiveness is the foundation for other-centered love.

DR. DAN B. ALLENDER,
BOLD LOVE

What Is Forgiveness?

Whatever the relationship, forgiveness is a truly healing gift for the people involved. In a marriage, the power of true forgiveness cannot be overstated.

Forgiveness is, at the same time, a pure, supernatural giving: the receiver doesn't deserve it; the giver wants nothing for it. It's not a *thanks*giving, because that's the return of one goodness for another. It's not a purchasing price, not even the price of marital peace, because that is hoping to buy one goodness with another. Forgiveness is not a good work which expects some reward in the end, because that motive focuses upon the giver, while this kind of giving must focus completely upon the spouse, the one receiving the gift, the one who sinned. The forgiver cannot say, "Because I have given something to you, now you must give something to me." That's no gift at all.

Rather, forgiveness is giving love when there is no reason to love and no guarantee that love will be returned. The spouse is simply not lovable right now! Forgiveness is repaying evil with kindness, doing all the things that love requires—even when you don't *feel* the love; for you can *do* love also in the desert days when you do not feel loving.

Only when a pure, unexpected, unreasonable, and undeserved gift-giving appears in the marriage does newness enter in and healing begin. This is grace. Only when the spouse has heard his sin, so that he might anticipate, under the law, some retribution, but receives instead the gestures of love—only then can he begin to change and grow in the same humility which his wife has shown him. Finally, gift-giving is the greatest sacrifice of all, for it is the complete "giving away" of one's self.

WALTER WANGERIN, JR., *As for Me and My House*

Steps of Forgiveness

First we are hurt, and feelings of anger may consume us. Then thoughts of how we can get revenge come creeping in. But only when we are ready to relinquish the hurt is there an opportunity for forgiveness and healing to begin.

Forgiveness demands we get in touch with our anger and bitterness—and get past the denial of built-up resentments. We cannot be bitter and be led by God at the same time. Unconsciously we may say, "I choose to react toward them with bitterness." We choose our attitude in any circumstance. Unfortunately, we seldom vent our anger at the person to whom it is intended, but rather family members and friends must bear the brunt of our outbursts.

Forgiveness is not always possible on our own. That's when we must pray, "God, in my own strength it is impossible for me to forgive. I am ready to be made willing to forgive this person. Help me find the strength to make the phone call or write the letter that will begin the healing process."

Total forgiveness means first we ask God for forgiveness of our poor attitude and seek his help (1 John 1:9). Then we must go to the other party and ask their forgiveness (James 5:16). And as we ask, we must be ready and willing to offer forgiveness (Matthew 6:14–15).

Forgiveness is a mark of a virtuous life. "Do not repay anyone evil for evil. Be careful to do what is right in the eyes of everybody. If it is possible, as far as it depends on you, live at peace with everyone. Do not take revenge, my friends, but leave room for God's wrath, for it is written: 'It is mine to avenge; I will repay,' says the Lord" (Romans 12:17–19 NIV).

It is only as we thank God for His forgiveness that we sense our anger and bitterness slipping away and are able to get on with the process of living.

Forgiveness Leads to Reconciliation

Forgiveness can be a critical issue among family members—especially around the holiday season.

Suppose all those people who are dreading the holidays could forgive the individuals who wounded them and those who have perpetrated the hurts would be willing to apologize and ask for forgiveness? Wouldn't that remove the spectre-like overtones which often obscure the joy of the holidays?

It may seem to be an overly simplistic solution, but the Scriptures clearly teach that forgiveness is essential to reconciliation and restoration of broken relationships.

Of course, it is not in our power to cause another person to apologize and seek forgiveness from us. But conducting our own personal "attitude check-up" is something each of us can and should do. We should be as diligent about getting rid of unforgiveness in our hearts as a cardiologist would be about dealing with plaque in our arteries. One is as great a threat to our spiritual health as the other is to our physical health.

How tragic to hear of a young man being stricken in the prime of life with deadly heart disease, often a treatable condition he was unaware of. Even more tragic is a person of any age who has allowed unforgiveness to corrode his soul and poison his spirit, while defending his right to bear a grudge. That kind of corrosion kills one's spiritual life and also affects one's physical well-being.

RUTHANNE GARLOCK, *HOW TO FORGIVE YOUR CHILDREN*

I will forgive their iniquity, and I will remember their sin no more. JEREMIAH 31:34 KJV

An apology is a friendship preserver, an antidote for hatred, never a sign of weakness; it costs nothing but one's pride, always saves more than it costs, and is a device needed in every home.

AUTHOR UNKNOWN

Praise the Lord, I tell myself, and never forget the good things he does for me. He forgives all my sins and heals all my diseases. He ransoms me from death and surrounds me with love and tender mercies.

PSALM 103:2–4 NLT

Forgiveness, No Matter What

If Jesus could forgive, given what was done to him, shouldn't we follow suit?

As Jesus died in excruciating pain on the cross, he had much to resent. The envious and paranoid religious leaders had stalked him at length, arrested him on a trumped-up charge, forced him to undergo the injustice of a "kangaroo court," and sentenced him to death. He was then brutally beaten before being made to carry his own cross to the hill where the death sentence would be carried out—in the company of two hardened criminals.

Truly, it was a horrible death! Cruxifixion produced intense suffering. First, driving nails through the hands and feet attached the person's body to the cross. Besides the unending, searing pain of those wounds, the weight of the body pulled the limbs out of joint. That made it extremely difficult to breathe and caused the internal organs to begin to collapse on each other. In the end, most died of asphyxiation.

Roman citizens did not usually experience this cruel and lingering form of death. It was a symbol of brute power of the ruling class over the masses.

Yes, Jesus had plenty to resent, if he chose to do so. But he did not. Rather, as he hung on that hideous cross, he was primarily concerned with exactly the opposite: forgiveness. He asked his heavenly Father to forgive the very people who had unjustly done this to him.

From the cross, Jesus said: "Father, forgive them, for they do not know what they are doing." As hard as it may be to fathom, sometimes one person can be grievously hurt by someone else's actions or words without that other person knowing. At other times, as with Jesus, those involved knew their actions were serious. Yet, they had absolutely no idea how serious. They had executed Jesus, the Son of God, who was completely innocent of any of the charges leveled against him.

The Forgiving Life

It takes both the grace of God and an act of our will to purposely forget when we've been wronged.

Develop the fine art of forgetting petty wrongs and unkind acts. "Be kind to one another, tenderhearted, forgiving each other," Paul urged the Christians at Ephesus (4:32 NASB). A friend of Clara Barton, founder of the American Red Cross, once reminded Clara of an especially cruel thing done to her years before. "Don't you remember it?" her friend asked. "No," came the reply, "but I do distinctly remember forgetting it."

No one can be free and happy by harboring grudges. "Seek peace and pursue it" is good advice. Long before modern psychology determined that unresolved anger has the potential of making one physically ill, the Bible offered healthy words: "See to it . . . that no root of bitterness springing up causes trouble" (Hebrews 12:15 NASB).

EDWARD I. HAYES, *THE FOCUSED LIFE*

Generosity

We all have numerous resources from which to share. Having a "generous spirit" does not mean simply giving money. Time is another precious commodity, and generous volunteers enable many organizations to function well: hospitals, schools, missions, animal shelters, community centers, nursing homes, child-care centers, churches—and the list goes on. Look around. What do you have to share? A "spirit of generosity" means open-handedly giving time, energy, and creativity, as well as monetary resources. Great is the reward of the person who generously gives whatever he or she has to help others.

> *A generous man will prosper; he who refreshes others will himself be refreshed.*
>
> PROVERBS 11:25 NIV

Prove Your Faith with Generosity

True faith is demonstrated when we look for ways to be kind and generous to those in need.

Dear brothers and sisters, what's the use of saying you have faith if you don't prove it by your actions? That kind of faith can't save anyone. Suppose you see a brother or sister who needs food or clothing, and you say, "Well, good-bye and God bless you; stay warm and eat well"—but then you don't give that person any food or clothing. What good does that do?

So you see, it isn't enough just to have faith. Faith that doesn't show itself by good deeds is no faith at all—it is dead and useless.

JAMES 2:15–17 NLT

God Loves a Cheerful Giver

Remember this: Whoever sows sparingly will also reap sparingly, and whoever sows generously will also reap generously. Each man should give what he has decided in his heart to give, not reluctantly or under compulsion, for God loves a cheerful giver.

2 CORINTHIANS 9:6–7 NIV

One man gives freely, yet grows all the richer; another withholds what he should give, and only suffers want.

PROVERBS 11:24 RSV

A Poor Widow Gives All She Has

This story from the Holy Bible lets us know that giving a small amount graciously is much more important than giving a large amount grudgingly.

Then he went over to the collection boxes in the Temple and sat and watched as the crowds dropped in their money. Some who were rich put in large amounts. Then a poor widow came and dropped in two pennies. He called his disciples to him and remarked, "That poor widow has given more than all those rich men put together! For they gave a little of their extra fat, while she gave up her last penny" (Mark 12:41–44 LB).

In the Lord's eyes, this poor widow gave more than all the others put together, although her gift was by far the smallest. The value of a gift is not determined by its amount, but by the spirit in which it is given. A gift given grudgingly or for recognition loses its value. When you give, take heart—small gifts are more pleasing to God than large gifts when they are given out of gratitude.

LIFE APPLICATION BIBLE NOTES

The Reward of Generous People

All goes well for those who are generous, who lend freely and conduct their business fairly. Such people will not be overcome by evil circumstances. Those who are righteous will be long remembered. They do not fear bad news; they confidently trust the Lord to care for them. They are confident and fearless and can face their foes triumphantly. They give generously to those in need. Their good deeds will never be forgotten. They will have influence and honor.

PSALM 112:5–9 NLT

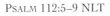 *It is more blessed to give than to receive.*

ACTS 20:35 KJV

God's Generous Character

In Scripture, God's laws reflect His generous character.

When you harvest your crops, do not harvest the grain along the edges of your fields, and do not pick up what the harvesters drop. It is the same with your grape crop—do not strip every last bunch of grapes from the vines, and do not pick up the grapes that fall to the ground. Leave them for the poor and the foreigners who live among you, for I, the Lord, am your God.

LEVITICUS 19:9–10 NLT

But if someone who is supposed to be a Christian has money enough to live well, and sees a brother in need, and won't help him—how can God's love be within him?

1 JOHN 3:17 LB

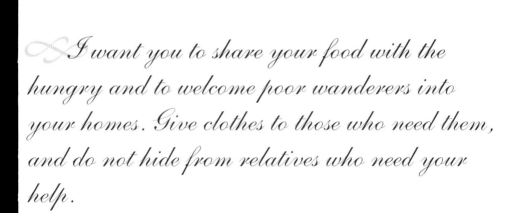

I want you to share your food with the hungry and to welcome poor wanderers into your homes. Give clothes to those who need them, and do not hide from relatives who need your help.

ISAIAH 58:7 NLT

Too Great a Gift to Keep

Some gifts are simply too special to keep to ourselves. We should share with everyone, including those we love.

My bounty is as boundless as the sea,
My love as deep; the more I give to thee,
The more I have, for both are infinite.

WILLIAM SHAKESPEARE

Is there any among you who, if your child asks for bread, will give a stone? Or if the child asks for a fish, will give a snake? If you then, who are evil, know how to give good gifts to

your children, how much more will your Father in heaven give good things to those who ask him!

MATTHEW 7:9–11

Every generous act of giving, with every perfect gift, is from above, coming down from the Father of lights.

JAMES 1:17 NRSV

Do What You Can

This little poem was written for the Lend-a-Hand Society. It serves as a good reminder that each of us can make a difference in our own way.

I am only one,
But still I am one.
I cannot do everything,
But still I can do something;
And because I cannot do everything
I will not refuse to do the something that
I can do.

EDWARD EVERETT HALE

Be Always Giving

All earthly creatures have a responsibility to give. Plants, animals, even bodies of water, all work together to create a balanced environment. We, too, must do our fair share.

The sun gives ever; so the earth —
What it can give so much 'tis worth;
The ocean gives in many ways —
Gives baths, gives fishes, rivers, bays;
So, too, the air, it gives us breath
When it stops giving, comes in death.
   Give, give, be always giving;
   Who gives not is not living;
     The more you give
     The more you live.

God's love hath in us wealth unheaped
Only by giving it is reaped;
The body withers, and the mind
Is pent up by a selfish rind.
Give strength, give thought, give deeds, give pelf
Give love, give tears, and give thyself.
   Give, give, be always giving,
   Who gives not is not living;
     The more we give
     The more we live.

AUTHOR UNKNOWN

He Gave His All

God compels us all to give of ourselves in different ways. For some people that may even mean giving the ultimate sacrifice of life.

Dr. Paul Carlson, the martyred medical servant of the people of Congo, was a college classmate and friend of mine. We had studied together, traveled together and in general kept in contact with each other for some time before he went to Africa.

Answering the call of the United Nations to furnish desperately needed medical help at the time of Congo's independence and revolution, Paul dedicated himself to do the obviously loving thing. He went to Africa because he was prepared to alleviate the existing need. A godly compulsion to give all of himself characterized his life.

After a couple of years, Paul's work, and that of a medical student assistant, caught the attention of a leading magazine, and a major news feature and picture story was prepared for publication. But as he was assisting the suffering, the great uprising occurred. He was captured by Congolese rebels, the Simbas, who claimed he was a foreign agent. While he was held prisoner in Stanleyville, thousands of us prayed impatiently for his release. After all, the rebels were not known for humanitarian behavior. When he and other prisoners were not released, rescue operations began. Planes were sent in an attempt to return as many captives as possible to safety. When the planes landed, the prisoners broke for freedom. But Paul's life ended in a hail of machine-gun bullets.

Immediately the story and pictures of his work, and the message of the supreme love of God for man that motivated him, was flashed throughout the world. Of his life one television commentator said, "Paul asked only for the opportunity to give, and it cost him his life."

The motivation and inspiration of his work were not lost, however. Today a medical foundation in the Congo continues Paul's selfless giving.

LLOYD H. AHLEM, *Do I Have To Be Me?*

149

Every man shall give as he is able, according to the blessing of the Lord thy God which he hath given thee.

DEUTERONOMY 16:17 KJV

When you help the poor you are lending to the Lord—and he pays wonderful interest on your loan!

PROVERBS 19:17 LB

Becoming a Generous Giver

To become truly generous in spirit, we must change the way we think about our possessions.

When we say, "Please enter—my house is your house, my joy is your joy, my sadness is your sadness and my life is your life," we have nothing to defend, since we have nothing to lose but all to give. Turning the other cheek means showing our enemies that they can only be our enemies while supposing that we are anxiously clinging to our private property, whatever it is: our knowledge, our good name, our land, our money, or the many objects we have collected around us. But who will be our robber when everything

he wants to steal from us becomes our gift to him? Who can lie to us, when only the truth will serve him well? Who wants to sneak into our back door, when our front door is wide open?

HENRI J. M. NOUWEN, *REACHING OUT*

God gave because He is love. It was the best He had to offer. The supreme gift. The total gift. In the person of His Son, He gave Himself.

What can I give Him,
Poor as I am?
If I were a shepherd
I would bring a lamb,
If I were a Wise Man
I would do my part,
Yet what can I give Him,
Give my heart.

CHRISTINA GEORGINA ROSSETTI

Instead of a gem or a flower, cast the gift of a lovely thought into the heart of a friend. GEORGE MACDONALD

The compassionate person builds up his own reservoir of peace, confidence, creativity, excitement, and resourcefulness and then generously shares it all as an encourager of others.

Give What You Have

Be it health or be it leisure,
    Be it skill we have to give,
Still in spending it for others
    Christians only really live.

Not in having or receiving,
    But in giving, there is bliss;
He who has no other pleasure
    Ever may rejoice in this.

AUTHOR UNKNOWN

All our opportunities, abilities, and resources come from God. They are given to us to hold in sacred trust for Him. Cooperating with God will permit us to generously pass on to others some of the many blessings from His rich storehouse.

Integrity

When we think of integrity, we think of someone who is honorable and trustworthy—a person who keeps their word and guards their reputation. To be called a man or woman of integrity is a high compliment. Such a person knows the difference between right and wrong and diligently pursues doing right, no matter what the obstacles. Jesus provides the best example of a man of integrity; He was not swayed by outer influences but lived a life above reproach. Integrity comes not just from the pursuit of right living, but the pursuit of God, which leads to right living.

Integrity: The Ultimate Virtue

Do we prize integrity above the tangible things in life? Are we concerned with being what we say we are? To become a person of integrity is a high calling and one worth pursuing.

The dictionary uses words such as *whole* and *complete* to describe what integrity means. *To borrow a modern expression, a man with integrity "has his act together."* There are no loose ends that threaten his reputation.

Recently I ran across a full-page ad for an international relief organization. The picture shows a young child—perhaps from Central America or possibly Asia—writing at her desk. The ad copy contains the following sentence: "Integrity. It's as simple as being what you say you are." That strikes me as an excellent definition of integrity. It means being what you say you are—*all* the time and in *every* situation.

To be called a man of integrity is the highest possible compliment. Several years ago my older brother took me to visit a cemetery outside Florence, Alabama, near the remains of an antebellum mansion called Forks of Cypress. The mansion was built in the 1820s by James Jackson, an early settler of northwest Alabama. My brother and I walked among the ruins of the mansion and then crossed the country road into the dense forest on the other side. After a quarter of a mile we found the Jackson family cemetery. There is no sign marking the spot, only a five-foot-high stone wall surrounding about fifty graves. Inside we found a tall marker over James Jackson's grave, with a long inscription extolling his virtues, which were many.

As I walked along, my eyes fas-

tened on the marker for one of his sons, William Moore Jackson. There was his name, the dates 1824–1891, and this simple five-word epitaph: "A man of unquestioned integrity."

Five words to sum up an entire life. Sixty-plus years distilled into five words. But, oh, what truth they tell.

"A man of unquestioned integrity." I cannot think of a better tribute. Then the thought came: "What will they put on my tombstone?"

I'm not sure what anyone will write on my tombstone. But I wouldn't mind if someone felt I deserved those five words.

RAY PRITCHARD, *THE ABC'S OF WISDOM*

Integrity Defined

A person of integrity is concerned not just with doing right but with right motives and right thinking.

Integrity is a wholesome or moral completeness, and is characteristic of a person whose life reflects the life of Jesus Christ. Integrity demonstrates the inner person — the motive behind the act. . . . Integrity encompasses all of what we do and are — speech, motives, and actions. A mature Christian walks in integrity, inwardly and outwardly.

JERRY WHITE, *HONESTY, MORALITY & CONSCIENCE*

Integrity and Responsibility

Many view saying "I was wrong" or "I need help" as signs of weakness. Only when we are willing to say these things are we taking steps toward true strength.

Integrity and responsibility go together.
People of integrity take responsibility
   rather than blaming others for their wrong behavior.
A person of integrity is not afraid to say,
   "I was wrong" and "Will you forgive me?"
   He or she has the courage to say, "I need help.
   I can't make it alone."
People of integrity
   are not afraid to tell others of their weaknesses,
and they discover ways to conquer them.

A Call to Integrity

People of integrity keep the promises they make. They are true to their word whether in business, their family lives, or in their relationship with God.

We have a unique opportunity today, the chance to stand up, be counted, and give men who have chosen a different road an alternative before it's too late. We need to recapture the spiritual climate in our own homes and cultivate a heart for other men. Our homes, men, are about to collapse. The homes we live in are coming apart at the seams. But we can't just worry about our own homes. We've got to foster regard and concern for the homes around us. Together we must stand up and be counted for Almighty God.

To accomplish all this, to till the rough ground of this hostile culture and plant some new seeds for Christ, each of us must commit to model what I call the three non-negotiables of manhood: integrity, commitment and action.

If you were to take the word integrity and reduce it to its simplest terms you'd conclude that a man of integrity is a promise keeper. He's a guy who, when he says something, can be trusted. When he gives his word, you can take it to the bank. His word is good.

BILL MCCARTNEY, *WHAT MAKES A MAN?*

Integrity in Youth

Parents teach children integrity by what they do, not what they say. Organizations like the Girl Scouts and Boy Scouts attempt to instill integrity in children, so they will grow up honorably.

The Girl Scout Law

I will do my best to be
    honest and fair,
    friendly and helpful,
    considerate and caring,
    courageous and strong, and
    responsible for what I say and do,
and to
    respect myself and others,
    respect authority,
    use resources wisely,
    make the world a better place, and
    be a sister to every Girl Scout.

JUNIOR GIRL SCOUT HANDBOOK

On My Honor

Our honor is our good name, our public esteem, our reputation. God wants us to act honorably and to do the right thing even if no one sees us—even if others refuse to do right.

The Girl Scout Promise

On my honor, I will try:
    To serve God and my country,
    To help people at all times,
    And to live by the Girl Scout Law.

JUNIOR GIRL SCOUT HANDBOOK

Learning Integrity

When we see people of integrity, one comment we can make about them is that they have grown up. They no longer react to life in the ways they did as a child. They have allowed God to raise them above that.

Few men know how to live. We grow up at random carrying into mature life the merely animal methods and motives which we had as little children. And it does not occur to us that all this must be changed, that much of it must be reversed; that life is the finest of Fine Arts; that it has to be learned with lifelong patience, and that the years of our pilgrimage are all too short to master it triumphantly.

Yet this is what Christianity is for—to teach men THE ART OF LIFE.

And its whole curriculum lies in one word—"Learn of me." Unlike most education, this is almost purely personal; it is not to be had from books, or lectures or creeds or doctrines. It is a study from the life. Christ never said much in mere words about the Christian graces. He lived them, He was them. Yet we do not merely copy Him. We learn His art by living with Him, like the old apprentices with their masters.

HENRY DRUMMOND,
THE GREATEST THING IN THE WORLD

People Notice a Person of Integrity

When a person of integrity is in a position of leadership, people may notice something "different" about them. This provides an opportunity for them to point to God as the source of their integrity.

When asked if he thought a year ago, when the team was languishing in its usual misery, if this turnaround was possible, he said he relied on his religious faith.

This would sound hokey out of anybody's mouth but Tony

Dungy's. He isn't a football coach. He's a gentleman. In a game driven only by money and muscle, in a sport that has warped the culture, he is so different that he can strike you as weird.

On Monday, he didn't hype himself. He didn't jump up and down. He talked about how nice it was to be stopped at the mall by well-wishers.

I say this with some discomfort, as one of those people who raised their voices against giving Dungy's boss the store, and a new stadium, too.

All those columns contained one question: Wasn't anything else more important than keeping a football team for a community with so many great and crying needs?

The answer was, and is, yes. Schools, parks, law and order, we recite the litany instantly.

That rare commodity, values, is also on the list.

You can't buy them.

But you can get Tony Dungy. The man embodies the best ones. He's focused. He's soft-spoken. He's steady. The first thing you see when you meet him is not an ego the size of Montana. The next thing you think is that every school child should meet him. And his wife. And his family.

It's easy, of course, to say this now that he's made the Bucs rise from the dead. So easy the words sound cheap.

But football's values are so screwy, he got points taken off during the commentators' reviews for not going bonkers on the sidelines Sunday night. Football's values are so screwy that, if the Bucs blow what they've begun, critics will say Tony Dungy isn't man enough for the job. Isn't mean and violent enough.

Football's values are our values, and our values also made a very qualified man wait longer than he should have to become a coach, because he came in the wrong color.

Tony Dungy's values are different. The miracle may continue, or the Bucs may go down in flames. Either way, we'll be watching a man of character at work.

MARY JO MELONE, "TORNADO OF BUCS HYPE SWIRLS PAST A QUIET PILLAR"

How far that little candle throws his beams! So shines a good deed in a naughty world.

WILLIAM SHAKESPEARE,
THE MERCHANT OF VENICE

Refusing to Compromise

When we make a decision to do right, there will most likely be opposition. It is a test of a person's integrity to stand firm during those trying times, as is evident from the true story below.

Eric said simply but with great firmness, "I'm afraid there are no ways, sir." The others stared at him. "I cannot run on the Sabbath and that's final. . . ."

"Don't be impertinent, Liddell," snapped Lord Adogan.

"The impertinence lies, sir, with those who seek to influence a man to deny his beliefs. God made countries and God makes kings

and the rules by which they govern," said Eric. "Those rules say the Sabbath is His and I for one intend to keep it that way. . . ."

Suddenly there was an interruption.

A uniformed attendant announced, "Lord Lindsay."

Andy hurried in, glanced quickly round, and went and stood by Eric. The Prince and the others gave him friendly looks. Not only was the young Lord one of them, an artistocrat himself, but he had won a silver medal.

"Your Highness, Cadogan, Gentlemen," he said, "I do apologize for barging in like this. The fact is I'm fully aware of Eric's dilemma, and I wonder if I could be so bold as to suggest a possible

solution. The 400 meters, it's on Thursday. I've already got my medal, so why don't you let Eric take my place in the 400 meters?"

"I think that's a splendid idea," said the Duke of Sutherland.

Eric turned to Andy.

"Andy, I . . . ." It embarrassed him that Andy was sacrificing his own chance at another Olympic medal.

Andy grinned. "A pleasure, old chap, just to see you run."

Eric decided he couldn't turn down such a sporting offer. "Then 'Aye' it is. . . ."

Lord Birkenhead whispered to the Duke of Sutherland, "Thank God for Lindsay, George. I thought the lad had us beaten."

"He did have us beaten," the Duke said quietly, "And thank God he did."

"I don't follow, George."

"The 'lad,' as you call him, is a true man of principle and a true athlete. His speed is a mere extension of his life, its force. We sought to sever his running from himself."

"For his country's sake."

"No sake is worth that," said the Duke, "Least of all a guilty national pride."

W. J. WEATHERBY, *CHARIOTS OF FIRE*

The Testing of Convictions

It is one thing to say, "I believe this is the right action." It is quite another to do the right thing when people oppose us and when doing right seems impossible.

We need to pass on to our children and remind ourselves that if we have deep convictions—convictions that have not just been handed to us, but that have been seared into our souls through difficult battles won—those convictions will be tested. They will be tried in the fires of outside pressures. I am not certain that a conviction is a worthwhile one if it is not tested and tried in the refining fires of life experiences and human opposition.

Integrity Is Threatened by Temptation

*Temptations we face fall into three categories. We are tempted sensually—
to inappropriately feed the desires of our physical bodies. We are tempted
to presume upon the grace of God—to do things our way, believing God
will rescue us. We are tempted in the area of gaining power and control.*

Then Satan tempted him to get food by changing stones into loaves of
bread.

"It will prove you are the Son of God," he said.

But Jesus told him, "No! For the Scriptures tell us that bread won't
feed men's souls: obe-
dience to every word
of God is what we
need."

Then Satan took
him to Jerusalem to
the roof of the Temple.
"Jump off," he said,
"and prove you are the
Son of God; for the
Scriptures declare,
'God will send his
angels to keep you
from harm,'...

they will prevent you from smashing on the rocks below."

Jesus retorted, "It also says not to put the Lord your God to a foolish test!"

Next Satan took him to the peak of a very high mountain and
showed him the nations of the world and all their glory. "I'll give it all to
you," he said, "if you will only kneel and worship me."

"Get out of here, Satan," Jesus told him. "The Scriptures say, 'Worship only the Lord God. Obey only him.'"

MATTHEW 4:3–10 LB

Standing Against Temptation

It is not true that people of integrity are not tempted. They are just ready for it and know what to do when it happens. The key is depending on God rather than on their own strength to resist temptation.

Therefore let him who thinks he stands take heed lest he fall. No temptation has overtaken you but such as is common to man; and God is faithful, who will not allow you to be tempted beyond what you are able, but with the temptation will provide the way of escape also, that you may be able to endure it.

1 Corinthians 10:12–13 NASB

An Uphill Climb

No one says that integrity is easy. Often it is a strain, but in the end it's worth the struggle.

The hill, though high, I covet to
    ascend,
The difficult will not me offend;
For I perceive the way to life lies
    here.
Come, pluck up heart, let's neither
    faint nor fear;
Better, though difficult, the right
    way to go,
Then wrong, though easy, where
    the end is woe.

John Bunyan, *Pilgrim's Progress*

A man of integrity is not one who never does anything wrong, but one who is grieved each time he does and desires to make things right.

Integrity Under Pressure

One test of people's character is what they do in hard times — what they do under pressure. Do they compromise their integrity using excuses for their wrong choices? Or do they have the courage to do the right thing no matter what they come up against?

Bad company corrupts good character.

1 CORINTHIANS 15:33 NIV

Set Your Heart to Do Right

...you don't have to think about doing the right thing. If you're for the right thing, then you do it without thinking.

Maya Angelou, *I Know Why the Caged Bird Sings*

Maintaining Integrity

This excerpt from a letter dated July 17, 1861, is from a father to his only son, an infantry soldier during the Civil War.

Try to maintain your Christian profession among your comrades. I need not caution you against strong drink as useless and hurtful, nor against profanity, so common among soldiers. Both these practices you abhor. Aim to take at once a decided stand for God. If practicable have prayers regularly in your tent, or unite with fellow-disciples in prayer-meetings in the camp. Should preaching be accessible, always be a hearer. Let the world know that you are a Christian. Read a chapter in the New Testament, which your mother gave you, every morning and evening, when you can, and engage in secret prayer to God for his holy Spirit to guide and sustain you. I would rather hear of your death than of the shipwreck of your faith and good conscience.

Carlton McCarthy, *Soldier Life*

Courage to Do Right

It's easy to go along with others, especially when those "others" are trusted friends. But if we are willing to take a stand for what is right, we can help set a standard for others.

The judge looked down from his bench and, in a somber voice, declared, "Mr. Wilson, this is your day of reckoning!" Then he sentenced him to seven and one-half years in federal prison.

In response, Wilson's lawyer requested that he be allowed a few minutes with his family and friends before surrendering to the authorities.

The judge replied, "Mr. Wilson is going to be taken by the marshals right now. You should have thought of that before."

Wilson was one of four California men convicted of financial fraud and sentenced to prison in that particular case. Five men were originally investigated, but the fifth, Mark Jacobs, was not arrested and charged.

Jacobs had been invited to join the financial scheme by four friends (the men sent to jail) in a weekly Bible study. They had assured him their plan was totally legal. Yet something inside him said it wasn't right. While it was hard to say no to good friends, he chose to go with his conscience and tell them he wouldn't participate.

The lawyers for the four convicted men pleaded with the judge that their clients made mistakes of poor judgment. They were good men who loved their wives and kids, gave to charities, and were active in their churches. Their crime involved a "gray" area, crossing a line that wasn't clear.

The judge disagreed. "It is not hard to determine where the line is," he said. "The guy who drew the line is Mark Jacobs. He knew what was right and what was wrong, and he didn't hesitate. Hopefully, now we will have fewer people who are willing to walk up to the line and dabble with going over the line. We will have people like Mr. Jacobs who wouldn't touch this thing with a ten-foot pole."

GARY J. OLIVER, PH.D.,
SEVEN PROMISES OF A PROMISE KEEPER

The righteous man walks in his integrity;
His children are blessed after him.

PROVERBS 20:7 NKJV

Be advised that every time you avoid doing
right, you increase your disposition to do wrong.

ANONYMOUS

To Be an Honorable Man

It's not easy to be a person of honor and integrity. Those around may not follow suit, and one might have to stand alone. But doing this will help a person mature, both mentally and spiritually.

If

If you can keep your head when all
    about you
Are losing theirs and blaming it on you;
If you can trust yourself when all men
    doubt you,
But make allowance for their doubting too;
If you can wait and not be tired of waiting,
Or, being lied about, don't deal in lies,
Or, being hated, don't give way to hating,
And yet don't look too good, nor talk too
    wise;

If you can dream — and not make dreams
    your master;
If you can think — and not make thoughts
    your aim;
If you can meet with triumph and disaster
And treat these two impostors just the same;
If you can bear to hear the truth you've
    spoken
Twisted by knaves to make a trap for fools,
Or watch the things you gave your life to
    broken,
And stoop and build 'em up with wornout
    tools;

If you can make one heap of all your
    winnings
And risk it on one turn of pitch-and-toss,
And lose, and start again at your beginnings
And never breathe a word about your loss;
If you can force your heart and nerve and
    sinew
To serve your turn long after they are gone,
And so hold on when there is nothing in you
Except the Will which says to them:
    "Hold on";

If you can talk with crowds and keep your
    virtue,
Or walk with kings—nor lose the common
    touch;
If neither foes nor loving friends can hurt you;
If all men count with you, but none too much;
If you can fill the unforgiving minute
With sixty seconds' worth of distance run—
Yours is the Earth and everything that's in it,
And—which is more—you'll be a Man, my
    son!

       RUDYARD KIPLING

Character Developed Through Adversity

When life doesn't go according to our plan, and calamity strikes, our true character is revealed. How we handle adversity signals what kind of person we are deep inside.

When I think of people I admire, I think of Michael. When he was seventeen, while on a mission trip with the church youth group, he over-rotated a flip while practicing a gymnastics routine and landed on his face. He broke his neck, and he has not taken a step since.

What has amazed me about Michael is his attitude about being in a wheelchair, paralyzed from the chest down with limited use of his hands. When I have seen him at church, I have not heard him complain or give in to self-pity. Instead he always seems to be upbeat and positive. I have not seen him get impatient or lose his temper in frustration as I would at having to ask people for help all the time and having to do things at a slower pace than is normal for such a young person.

"It's not like I don't miss being able to run around," he said to a local newspaper reporter who wrote an article about him when he graduated from St. Petersburg Junior College, after giving a speech from his wheelchair to 800 members of his graduating class. "I miss that, and there are times that I get down, times that I get so fed up, so tired of having to depend on people to do the same old stuff for me over and over."

Lately I'm one of the people that Michael depends on. He has been asking me to go to his house, drive his van down to his college, the University of South Florida, which is about 30 minutes away, and bring him home one day a week. I thought I might see the negative side of Michael getting this up close and personal. But I haven't. He didn't even get impatient with me when he had to explain time after time how to correctly connect and tighten the straps that hold his wheelchair

securely in place in the van. In fact, each time I drive him home, he cheers and encourages me and my 17-year-old daughter who sometimes comes along. He thinks I'm doing him a favor and helping him out, but some days I wonder who's helping whom.

Why is it that someone like Michael can have his character so enriched by adversity while others' lives seem destroyed by it? He claims it is his faith in God. Out of that faith comes his acceptance of his disability—that this is the life God has given him, and he must embrace it and make the best of it. And he is doing just that. He has told his story on television, and he speaks to young people, encourag-ing them to hang in there. When I asked him recently what his career goals are, he said, "I just want to help people." He's doing that already, in more ways than he knows.

On November 10, 1997, Michael turned 21 years old. An interesting coincidence is that this date was also the 222nd birthday of the United States Marine Corps—an organization that prides itself on looking for "a few good men." Some in society believe that when a male turns 21, he officially reaches manhood. I believe Michael has been a man—a *good* man (God's definition, not the Marines')—for a while now.

Happy Birthday, Michael!

A Prayer for Allegiance to God

Deliver me, O God, from a slothful mind, from all lukewarmness, and all dejection of spirit. I know these can-not but deaden my love to you; mer-cifully free my heart from them, and give me a lively, zealous, active, and cheerful spirit, that I may vigor-ously perform whatever you command, thankfully suffer whatever you choose for me, and be ever ardent to obey in all things your holy love.

JOHN WESLEY

People of Integrity Do Soul Searching

People of high character examine their souls to see if there is anything amiss. Then they take steps to correct the flaws.

Have you explored your soul? It is not too late to do so. The pursuit is quite rewarding....

It would be a great thing to feel that one had contrived to find out exactly what one's soul is good for; what strains and stresses it can endure; how well equipped it is for the strange adventure upon which it is ultimately to set forth; how fit it is to stand in the white light that beats against the throne of God.

LLOYD C. DOUGLAS,
THE LIVING FAITH

Integrity without knowledge is weak and useless, and knowledge without integrity is dangerous and dreadful.

SAMUEL JOHNSON

Right and Wrong Remain the Same

Some would like to believe that the times we live in define what is right and what is wrong. There are always things we shouldn't do in any society. People of integrity are able to resist those wrongs instead of finding ways to call them right and indulging themselves.

To an increasing number of people, breaking certain "insignificant" laws doesn't matter. But when you think about it, lawbreakers break down any society, little by little.

However, in the spiritual realm, those who break God's laws, even the seemingly "insignificant" ones, will be considered at the bottom of the ladder in God's kingdom.

Sadly, law-abiding citizens in our society often get overlooked. Happily, that is not the case in God's kingdom. In the Lord's evaluation of what really matters for time and

eternity, obedience to his standards and passing on that reverence to others is considered true greatness. You don't have to be the best to be great in God's eyes. All it takes is an attitude of obedience to him and a willingness to model this attitude to others.

A Desire to Do Right

A person of integrity desires to keep God's laws and is willing to be examined by Him. Such a person deliberately seeks out good company.

I have tried to keep your laws and have trusted you without wavering. Cross-examine me, O Lord, and see that this is so; test my motives and affections too. For I have taken your lovingkindness and your truth as my ideals. I do not have fellowship with tricky, two-faced men; they are false and hypocritical. I hate the sinners' hangouts and refuse to enter them.

PSALM 26:1–5 LB

Do to others as you would have them do to you.

LUKE 6:31 NIV

Peace

*P*eace describes the state of being we all desire to have. The word "peace" brings to mind "the absence of war." It evokes images of people getting along with one another and living together in harmony. A similar sense comes from having inner peace: a quality of internal rest and calm. But neither kind of peace can be had without paying the price for it: We must release everything to God. We know that we've acquired true peace if, when things are chaotic all around us, we can be calm and trust in the One of whom the Scriptures say, "He Himself is our peace . . . ."

Peace

Areas of Peace

God wants us to know peace in every area of our lives—peace in our daily work, our business, our family, our soul. The key to letting peace enter in is to invite God into each of these areas daily.

Peace in daily work is the consciousness of health and ability to spare so that when one's tasks are done there is a margin all around. Peace in business is the consciousness of capital and plenty, so that one need not fear what the day may bring. Peace in the family is the consciousness that, under all the strains inevitably incident to the running of a home, there is an unfailing wealth of love and devotion and fidelity to fall back upon. Peace in the soul is the consciousness that, however difficult life may be, we are not living it alone.

HARRY EMERSON FOSDICK,
TWELVE TESTS OF CHARACTER

From Fear to Peace

We don't want to be afraid, but sometimes we are. We look to God for answers, comfort, and peace.

The peace of God releases fear. Jesus wants to give us peace, an assurance that no matter what happens we are not alone. The peace that Jesus gives is the quiet confidence that God is with us. Even when trouble strikes, God is present. God is at work in all things, working for good, working for healing.

Each day we can take a moment to breathe in God's presence. As we inhale, we can say, "The peace of God is within me." As we exhale, we can say, "The peace of God is all around me." This is the deep peace of God that lets us walk through each day unafraid and knowing that God's peace can bear the day's troubles. Carry God's peace with you.

Peace

Peace—serene confidence, free from fears and agitating passions and moral conflicts.

2 PETER 3:14 AMPLIFIED

If it is possible, as far as it depends on you, live at peace with everyone.

ROMANS 12:18 NIV

Let Go of Anger — Embrace Peace

One of the greatest robbers of peace in our lives is anger. It affects our minds, our bodies, and our emotions. If we choose to let go of anger, we can embrace peace again.

Lord, I feel angry at so many people. Often I think my life would be peaceful if they would just do the right thing. I convince myself they are robbing me of peace, but at this moment I know it can be *my* choice to let go of anger and embrace peace. Staying angry at them for not living up to my expectations doesn't solve any problems — it just creates new ones. Please help me to remember that "anger does not bring about the righteous life that God desires" (James 1:20 NIV) — in me or in those at whom I'm angry. Give me strength to release them — over and over again if need be — so I can go back to that serene, tranquil place called "peace." In Jesus' name. Amen.

Peace

The World's Way of Seeking Peace

If we want peace with others, we need to let go of self-interest. Only then does peace become possible.

Jesus' way would be peace itself if we followed it. But men don't want to change as radically as that! They are still trying to make selfish greed work. In the peace negotiations, nations have jostled for special privilege, and selfish business interests have tried to grab advantages that would be sure to make other men hate them. Senator Vandenberg wrote before the San Francisco Conference that nations were striving for "America first," "England first," "Russia first,"—the very attitude which has caused all wars. Peace cannot be permanent until we put "the whole world first." No part of the world, whether America or England or Russia, or any business enterprise, is as important as the welfare of all. "Thy kingdom come on earth" is not only Christian, it is the only possible road to lasting peace.

FRANK C. LAUBACH, *PRAYER: THE MIGHTIEST FORCE IN THE WORLD*

Blessed are the peacemakers: for they shall be called the children of God.

MATTHEW 5:9 KJV

Becoming a Peacemaker

Can we find peace in a pill or in therapy? Or is it true that peace comes from God alone?

Where does peacemaking begin? How can we become peacemakers?

We have pointed out that peace can never come out of war. War is the sire of poverty, depression, suffering, and hatred—it has never given us permanent peace.

Can peace be discovered within ourselves? Freud has told us that peace is but a mental attitude. Cast off our phobias, shed our neuroses, and "bingo!"—we'll have the coveted peace men long for.

I respect psychiatry for what it can do. Unquestionably it has helped many. But it certainly is no satisfactory substitute for the peace which can only come from God. If psychiatry leaves God out, ultimately we shall see psychiatrists going to each other for treatment. There can be no peace until we find peace with God.

BILLY GRAHAM, *THE SECRET OF HAPPINESS*

Love and Peace

Do we really want peace the way God views peace? Perhaps we need to rethink our idea of what "peace" really is. God is always ready to give us true peace if we are willing to ask Him for it.

Will you end wars by asking men to trust men who evidently cannot be trusted? No. Teach them to love and trust God; then they will be able to love the men they cannot trust, and will dare to make peace with them, not trusting in them but in God....

Perhaps peace is not, after all, something you work for, or "fight for." It is indeed "fighting for peace" that starts all the wars.... Peace is something you have or you do not have. If you are yourself at peace, then there is at least *some* peace in the world. Then share your peace with everyone, and everyone will be at peace.

THOMAS MERTON, *THE TRUE SOLITUDE*

When a man's ways are pleasing to the Lord he makes even his enemies live at peace with him.

PROVERBS 16:7 NIV

Peace

*Peace hath her victories
No less renowned than War.*

JOHN MILTON, *To the Lord General Cromwell*

*There is an appointed time for everything.
And there is a time for every event under
heaven . . . A time for war, and a time for
peace.*

ECCLESIASTES 3:1, 8 NASB

Peaceful Thoughts

When we focus on the negative, peace eludes us. But positive thinking leads to peace.

Fix your thoughts on what is true and good and right. Think about things that are pure and lovely, and dwell on the fine, good things in others. Think about all you can praise God for and be glad about. Keep putting into practice all you learned from me and saw me doing, and the God of peace will be with you.

PHILIPPIANS 4:8–9 LB

Prayer Brings Peace

Instead of lugging around our cares, we can pray. Prayer opens the door to peace.

Don't worry about anything; instead, pray about everything; tell God your needs and don't forget to thank him for his answers. If you do this you will experience God's peace, which is far more wonderful than the human mind can understand. His peace will keep your thoughts and your hearts quiet and at rest as you trust in Christ Jesus.

PHILIPPIANS 4:6–7 LB

Peace Is Declared

The soul celebrates when a war ends, whether on the battlefield, in our homes, or on the job. At those times, peace seems like a brand-new, lovely thing.

The cries sound gradually fainter. The road drags on toilsomely. We are carrying a lot of stuff—a man must bring something back home with him. Clouds hang in the sky. During the afternoon the sun breaks through, and birch trees, now with only a few leaves left, hang mirrored in puddles of rain along the way. Soft blue haze is caught in the branches.

As I march on with pack and lowered head, by the side of the road I see an image of bright, silken trees reflected in the pools of rain. In the occasional mirrors they are displayed clearer than in reality. They get another light and in another way. Embedded there in the brown earth lies a span of sky, trees, depths and clearness. Suddenly I shiver. For the first time in many years I feel again that something is still beautiful, that this in all its simplicity is beautiful and pure, this image in the water pool before me—and in this thrill my heart leaps up. For a moment all that other falls away, and now, for the first time, I feel it; I see it; I comprehend it fully: Peace. The weight that nothing eased before now lifts at last. Something strange, something new flies up, a dove—a white dove. Trembling horizon, tremulous expectancy, first glimpse, presentiment, hope, exaltation, imminence: Peace.

Sudden panic, and I look around. There behind me on the stretchers my comrades are now lying and still they call. It is peace, yet they must die. But I, I am trembling with joy and am not ashamed.—And that is odd.

Because none can ever wholly feel what another suffers—is that the reason why wars perpetually recur?

ERICH MARIA REMARQUE, *THE ROAD BACK*

With Acceptance Comes Peace

We can decide to be at peace with the state of our lives. If we're constantly desiring more and better things and positions, rather than being contented with what we have, we'll never know true peace.

To enjoy a little happiness, to have a taste of heaven on earth, you must accept life, your own life, just as it is now. You must be at peace with your work, with the people around you, with their faults and their imperfections. You must be content with your husband, your wife, even if you now realize you did not marry the ideal husband or the ideal wife. (I don't believe they exist anyway.) You must be at peace with the size of your purse, your status in the community, with your face (which you did not choose yourself), with your home, your furniture, your clothes, with your own living standards—even if your neighbor's things are so much better and so much finer, so you think. Accept life. You only have one skin. You can't be born again in another one.

PHIL BOSMANS, *GIVE HAPPINESS A CHANCE*

The Lord blesses His people with peace.

PSALM 29:11 NIV

A Place to Find Peace

Sometimes we find a place where we can go and find peace. We listen to the sounds of nature and observe the beauty of God's creation, and we know He is still in control.

This is my ledge
of quiet,
my shelf of peace,
edged
by its crooked rails
holding back the beyond.
Above,
a hawk sails
high
to challenge clouds
trespassing
my plot of sky.
Below
in the valley,
remote and dim,

sounds
come and go,
a requiem
for quiet.
Here on my ledge,
quiet praise:
of birds,
crickets,
breeze—
in different ways;
and so do I—
for these:
my ledge of quiet,
my plot of sky:
for peace.

RUTH BELL GRAHAM,
RUTH BELL GRAHAM'S COLLECTED POEMS

Peace

Peace in the Midst of Tragedy

Sometimes we believe our souls can be at peace only if there is no outer turmoil. The wonder of God's peace is that even when the world around us is in confusion and our emotions are in a whirl, underneath it all we can know His peace.

When Mr. Moody and I were holding meetings in Edinburgh, in 1874, we heard the sad news of the loss of the French steamer, "Ville De Havre," on her return from America to France, with a large number of members of the Ecumenical Council whose meetings had been held in Philadelphia. On board the steamer was a Mrs. Spafford, with her four children. In mid-ocean a collision took place with a large sailing vessel, causing the steamer to sink in half an hour. Nearly all on board were lost. Mrs. Spafford got her children out of their berths and up on deck. On being told that the vessel would soon sink, she knelt down with her children in prayer, asking God that they might be saved if possible; or be made willing to die, if that was his will. In a few minutes the vessel sank to the bottom of the sea, and the children were lost. One of the sailors of the vessel, named Lockurn—whom I afterward met in Scotland—while rowing over the spot where the vessel disappeared, discovered Mrs. Spafford floating in the water. Ten days later she was landed at Cardiff, Wales. From there she cabled to her husband, a lawyer in Chicago, the message, "Saved alone." Mr. Spafford, who was a Christian, had the message framed and hung up in his office. He started immediately for England to bring his wife to Chicago. Mr. Moody left his meeting in Edinburgh and went to Liverpool to try to comfort the bereaved par-

:nts, and was greatly pleased to find that they were able to say: "It is vell; the will of God be done."

In 1876, when we returned to Chicago to work, I was entertained at he home of Mr. and Mrs. Spafford for a number of weeks. During that :ime Mr. Spafford wrote the hymn, "It is well with my soul," in commemoration of the death of his children.

IRA D. SANKEY, *SANKEY'S STORY OF THE GOSPEL HYMNS*

It Is Well with My Soul

When peace, like a river, attendeth my way.
When sorrows like sea billows roll;
Whatever my lot, thou hast taught me to say,
It is well, it is well with my soul.
It is well with my soul, it is well, it is well with my soul.

HORATIO G. SPAFFORD

Peace I leave with you: my peace I give to you; not as the world gives do I give to you. Let not your hearts be troubled, neither let them be afraid.

JOHN 14:27 RSV

The Vision of Peace

Peace will come only when we work together with ourselves and God to make it happen.

Picture God's peace as the real presence of his love throughout the universe. Peace is not just calmness; it is a vibrant commingling of our humanity, talents, and gifts. It is the reflection of the Spirit within each of us. Peace is unity glorying our diversity.

We often think of peace as a lack of disagreement. More specifically, it is the harmonious settlement of disagreements. When we respond to the struggles of others, offering them hope or a solution to their conflicts, we are working toward far more encompassing peace than we may think.

Most of us believe that "charity begins at home." We hope that by doing good among our own that goodness will spread out like concentric rings on the surface of a lake. And, if people pass their blessings along, that is true. Just for a moment, though, think of the lake water in reverse. Say you start from far outside of your home and the circles travel inward to the core. Wouldn't that encourage you to also act more globally?

Reflections on Peace

We all make plans for our lives and have an agenda we want to hold on to. Yet if we let go and let God be in charge, the result will bring us peace.

Peace is about releasing.
It's about opening my hand
and letting go of my plan,
my agenda, my demands
on God and other people
and even on myself.
It's about realizing
that every person
is as important as I am
in God's eyes.
It's remembering
I don't know everything
and I don't have solutions
to every problem.
It's about calling on
the One who does.

Kindness

We've all heard that "actions speak louder than words." And so it is with the Christian life. Like it or not, we affect others by what we say and do. The Bible admonishes us to "Never tire of loyalty and kindness. Hold these virtues tightly" (Proverbs 3:3 LB). As examples in "word and deed," we are instructed to "clothe yourselves with compassion, kindness, humility, gentleness and patience"(Colossians 3:12 NIV). Whether with friends, family, coworkers, or even total strangers, God wants us to always treat others with the utmost care and respect.

Since God chose you to be the holy people whom he loves, you must clothe yourselves with tenderhearted mercy, kindness, humility, gentleness, and patience.

Colossians 3:12 NLT

A Little Word

A little word in kindness spoken,
    A motion or a tear,
Has often healed the heart that's broken!
    And made a friend sincere.

A word—a look—has crushed to earth,
    Full many a budding flower,
Which had a smile but owned its birth,
    Would bless life's darkest hour.

Then deem it not an idle thing,
    A pleasant work to speak;
The face you wear, the thoughts you bring,
    A heart may heal or break.

Author Unknown

In response to all he has done for us, let us outdo each other in being helpful and kind to each other and in doing good.

HEBREWS 10:24 LB

Spontaneous Kindness

Always, Sir, set a high value on spontaneous kindness. He whose inclination prompts him to cultivate your friendship of his own accord will love you more than one whom you have been at pains to attach to you.

SAMUEL JOHNSON

Rules of Conduct

Do all the good you can,
By all the means you can,
In all the ways you can,
In all the places you can,
At all the times you can,
To all the people you can,
As long as ever you can.

JOHN WESLEY

Kindness

Show a little kindness —
    Help a brother on the way.
Show a little kindness —
    In all you do and say.
Show a little kindness —
    It will soon come back to you,
As everyone around you
    starts showing kindness, too!

I Shall Not Pass This Way Again

We often do not get a second chance at doing the good deed that we should have done but neglected to do in the first place. So if you see the chance to do something good— do it now!

Through this toilsome world, alas!
Once and only once I pass;
If a kindness I may show,
If a good deed I may do
To a suffering fellow man,
Let me do it while I can.
No delay, for it is plain
I shall not pass this way again.

AUTHOR UNKNOWN

Act Kindly

When our lives are changed by God's mercy, we are expected to show this same mercy in our dealings with others.

Talk and act like a person expecting to be judged by the Rule that sets us free. For if you refuse to act kindly, you can hardly expect to be treated kindly. Kind mercy wins over harsh judgment every time.

JAMES 2:12–14 THE MESSAGE

Too Kind!

I have wept in the night
For the shortness of sight
    That to somebody's need made
    me blind.
But I never have yet
Felt a tinge of regret
    For being a little too kind!

AUTHOR UNKNOWN

Simple Act of Kindness

Just one seemingly simple act of kindness can have far-reaching consequences. If we stop to help someone out, we might make their day—or even make a new friend.

It was late Saturday afternoon when the pleasant-looking young lady with shoulder-length chestnut hair caught my attention—or rather the ankle-to-knee purple wrap over her leg cast caught it.

She was walking slowly on her crutches down the sloping sidewalk leading to the post office.

I smiled at her as I reached for my car door. "That looks like a real pain," I called to her.

"You're right, it is," she chuckled. Then, reaching the bench in front of my car, she called back, "You wouldn't happen to have change for a $10 bill? I need to buy stamps from the machine."

"No, sorry. I only have a twenty," I replied as I closed the door and put my key into the ignition.

"Oh well, I'll just sit here until someone comes along."

Stop. Elaine, you dummy. What's keeping you from running across the street to get change for her? The message came emblazoned across my conscience.

She was shocked to see me reopen the car door and walk toward her. "I'll be happy to run and get change for you from the grocery store."

"Oh, you don't have to do that. Someone will probably come with change pretty soon," she replied.

"I'd like to, really...it'll just take a minute. Wait a minute. Let me check the machine, first."

It took only three quick steps to reach the post office door and see the big "Out of Order" sign taped to the stamp dispenser. "Sorry, but there are no stamps here. The machine is out of order again."

In the next couple of minutes we brainstormed other possibilities. But on our little Northwest U.S. island, there appeared to be no other place to buy stamps.

Wait, Elaine. What's wrong with looking in your purse and giving her yours? There it was again—the still, small voice.

She was still talking to me, "That figures. I've had nothing but bad luck since I moved here. I nearly froze to death in our winter storm. My landlord was in California, and I had no water or electric-ity. Then I had this accident, and now I can't even drive to get around for another 45 days. My psychic told me this was my unlucky line and I shouldn't live in the Northwest. And the whole country is so militaristic. People here aren't friendly. I'd better just move to another country."

I breathed a quick prayer for just the right words to respond. "Just a minute," I broke in. "I have stamps in my purse in the car. Let me get them."

"I have some change. I can buy one from you. Oh, and here's my lucky silver dollar. You can take that, too," she said.

"No. I don't need your money. Here—take three or four extra," I insisted as I tore several from the little book of stamps.

We chatted for a few more minutes, and I learned she lived less than a mile from me. She had also become a volunteer cat and dog walker at the Humane Society to help alleviate her loneliness.

Give her your business card. There it was again—the still, small voice.

I was getting more involved than I planned. Quickly I went back to the car and got the card with my phone number.

"Listen, Denise (now I knew her name), I live near you. Give me a call if you need a ride to town. I come in at least twice a day, and I'd be happy to swing by and pick you up."

By this time she was reading my business card ... Christian Writers Consultant, it said under my name. "Oh! No wonder— you're a Christian. The only other person to be nice to me this week was a Christian, Rev. Baker, pastor at the Baptist church."

Sitting on the bench beside her, my schedule no longer seemed to matter. We talked another 20 minutes before I really had to go.

"I'll call you. Can we get together next week?" she asked when I stood to leave.

"Of course," I said. And as I drove away, I was smiling, not just at her but with deep thankfulness for that still, small voice.

Kindness and Compassion:
In God's Words

Luke 6:35 NIV — But love your enemies, do good to them, and lend to them without expecting to get anything back. Then your reward will be great, and you will be sons of the Most High, because he is kind to the ungrateful and wicked.

1 Peter 2:3 LB — Now that you realize how kind the Lord has been to you, put away all evil, deception, envy, and fraud.

Ephesians 4:32 NIV — Be kind and compassionate to one another, forgiving each other, just as in Christ God forgave you.

Romans 2:4 NIV — Do you show contempt for the riches of his kindness, tolerance and patience, not realizing that God's kindness leads you toward repentance?

Ephesians 2:7 LB — And now God can always point to us as examples of how very, very rich his kindness is.

2 Corinthians 6:6 LB — We have proved ourselves to be what we claim by our wholesome lives and by our understanding of the Gospel and by our patience. We have been kind and truly loving and filled with the Holy Spirit.

1 Corinthians 13:4 NIV — Love is patient, love is kind. It does not envy, it does not boast, it is not proud.

Galatians 5:22–23 LB — But when the Holy Spirit controls our lives he will produce this kind of fruit in us: love, joy, peace, patience, kindness, goodness, faithfulness, gentleness and self-control.

Tender Hearts and Humble Minds

In God's kingdom, revenge is unacceptable. Therefore, we are admonished to pray for people rather than to insult, pay back, or get even with them.

Finally, all of you should be of one mind, full of sympathy toward each other, loving one another with tender hearts and humble minds. Don't repay evil for evil. Don't retaliate when people say unkind things about you. Instead, pay them back with a blessing. That is what God wants you to do, and he will bless you for it.

1 Peter 3:8–9 NLT

A friend is a
person with whom
I may be sincere.
Before him I may
think aloud.

A friend is the
first person who comes
in when the whole
world has gone out.

RALPH WALDO EMERSON

Treat your friends for what you know them to be. Regard no surfaces. Consider not what they did but what they intended.

HENRY DAVID THOREAU

We ought to help one another by our advice, and yet more by our good examples.

BROTHER LAWRENCE,
THE PRACTICE OF THE PRESENCE OF GOD

Pass It On

The best way to increase the happiness of ourselves and others is by spreading it around.

Have you had a kindness shown? Pass it on, pass it on!
'Twas not given for thee alone, Pass it on, pass it on!
Let it travel down the years, Let it wipe another's tears;
Till in heav'n the deed appears, Pass it on, pass it on!

Did you hear the loving word! Pass it on, pass it on!
Like the singing of a bird? Pass it on, pass it on!
Let its music live and grow, Let it cheer another's woe;
You have reaped what others sow, Pass it on, pass it on!

Have you found the heav'nly light? Pass it on, pass it on!
Souls are groping in the night, Daylight gone, daylight gone!
Hold your lighted lamp on high, Be a star in someone's sky,
He may live who else would die, Pass it on, pass it on!

Chorus:
Pass it on, pass it on!
Cheerful word or loving deed, Pass it on,
Live for self, you live in vain;
Live for Christ, you live again,
Live for him, with him you reign,
Pass it on, pass it on!

WM. J. KIRKPATRICK

The Lord is gracious, and full of compassion; slow to anger, and of great mercy. PSALM 145:8 KJV

Compassionate Listening

Are we tuning out
or tuning in—
what are our habits
of listening?
Do we really care
to share a part
when a troubled sister
bares her heart?
Do words rush out
when nothing should be said—
when all we should do
is listen instead?

A friend is always loyal, and a brother is born to help in time of need.

PROVERBS 17:17 NLT

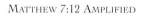So then, whatever you desire that others would do to and for you, even so do also to and for them, for this sums up the Law and the Prophets.

MATTHEW 7:12 AMPLIFIED

Remember that none of us has a responsibility to care for the whole world. Instead, our task is to care for the people who are closest to us. In this way we care for the world by starting with individuals, one at a time.

GARY R. COLLINS, *THE JOY OF CARING*

A Helping Heart

If I can stop one Heart from
    breaking
I shall not live in vain;
If I can ease one life the aching,
Or cool one pain,
Or help one fainting robin
Unto his nest again,
I shall not live in vain.

EMILY DICKINSON

Just One Need at a Time

*"He will encourage the
fainthearted, those tempted to
despair. He will see full justice given
to all who have been wronged. He
won't be satisfied until truth and
righteousness prevail throughout
the earth..." (Isaiah 42:3-4 LB).*

God,
I look around my community today
and I feel helpless.
The homeless, the hurting,
the needs each one represents
are more than I can handle.
But
You can do it.
You can meet each need.
Teach me.
Strengthen me and
use me to serve
as I reach out
to my neighbor
and meet
Just One Need at a Time!

Please Let Me Help You

"It is God himself who has made us what we are and given us new lives from Christ Jesus; and long ages ago he planned that we should spend these lives in helping others" *(Ephesians 2:10 LB).*

Please let me help you
however I can.
Long ages ago
it was God's plan
for me to serve,
to love and to share—
helping ease another's
burden of care.
So let me be
God's loving gift to you
because in serving others,
I am blessed, too.

Love is very patient and kind, never jealous or envious, never boastful or proud, never haughty or selfish or rude. Love does not demand its own way. It is not irritable or touchy. It does not hold grudges and will hardly even notice when others do it wrong. It is never glad about injustice, but rejoices whenever truth wins out.

1 CORINTHIANS 13:4–6 LB

Opportunities Don't Wait

*Seize the opportunity—it may never come
again. Today's the day to reach out and lend a
helping hand.*

Can't you see she's floundering—
your plans will surely wait.
If you don't offer help now,
tomorrow may be too late.

Sure—it's not convenient,
interruptions never are.
But when you stop to help another,
life is happier by far.

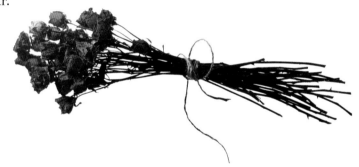

*Do not forget or neglect to do kindness and
good, to be generous and distribute and
contribute to the needy [of the church as
embodiment and proof of fellowship] , for such
sacrifices are well-pleasing to God.*

HEBREWS 13:16 AMPLIFIED

Take the Risk of Reaching Out

Often when we feel lonely or depressed, the best way to feel better is to give of ourselves. Not only will our own mood improve, but we'll also lift someone else's spirit, too!

It's well-known that Seattle gets a lot of rain. Rain, clouds, and the normal dark, miserable days tend to bring out my winter doldrums. Then it is easy to get preoccupied with "how I feel," "wish I had enough money to go find sun in Hawaii," "what's there to do in the rain," etc.

Shortly after moving to Seattle and not yet used to the long rainy season, I soon became tired of myself and my pity party. Looking for a book out of my library to bury myself in, I found a book that suggested that I help others in order to help myself.

The challenge was too obvious. It was true that the most meaningful experiences of my life had come when I dared to risk and reach out to others. When I am touching, smiling, helping, giving, and reaching beyond myself, I come much closer to being the person that God designed me to be.

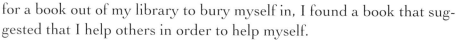

Thus speaketh the Lord of hosts, saying, Execute true judgment, and show mercy and compassions every man to his brother: And oppress not the widow, nor the fatherless, the stranger, nor the poor; and let none of you imagine evil against his brother in your heart.

ZECHARIAH 7:9–10 KJV

So don't get tired of doing what is good. Don't get discouraged and give up, for we will reap a harvest of blessing at the appropriate time. Whenever we have the opportunity, we should do good to everyone, especially to our Christian brothers and sisters.

GALATIANS 6:9–10 NLT

What Does It Mean to Care?

Of all the things that caring implies,
often what matters most is simply our presence.

What does it mean to care? Let me start by saying that the word *care* has become a very ambivalent word. When someone says: "I will take care of him!" it is more likely an announcement of an impending attack than of a tender compassion.... The basic meaning of care is: to grieve, to experience sorrow, to cry out with. I am very much struck by this background of the word *care* because we tend to look at caring as an attitude of the strong toward the weak, of the powerful toward the powerless, of the have's toward the have not's. And, in fact, we feel quite uncomfortable with an invitation to enter into someone's pain before doing something about it.

Still, when we honestly ask ourselves which persons in our lives mean the most to us, we often find that it is those who, instead of giving much advice, solutions, or cures, have chosen rather to share our pain and touch our wounds with a gentle and tender hand. The friend who can be silent with us in a moment of despair or confusion, who can stay with us in an hour of grief and bereavement, who can tolerate notknowing, not-curing, not-healing and face with us the reality of our powerlessness, that is the friend who cares.

You might remember moments in which you were called to be with a friend who had lost a wife or husband, child or parent. What can you say, do, or propose at such a moment? There is a strong inclination to say: "Don't cry; the one you loved is in the hands of God." "Don't be sad because there are so many good things left worth living for." But are we ready to really experience our powerlessness in the face of death and say: "I do not understand. I do not know what to do but I am here with you." Are we willing to **not** run away from the pain, to **not** get busy when there is nothing to do and instead stand rather in the face of death together with those who grieve?

The friend who cares makes it clear that whatever happens in the external world, being present to each other is what really matters.

HENRI J. M. NOUWEN, *OUT OF SOLITUDE*

The Tie That Binds

The following story is told about the origin of the beloved hymn "Blest Be the Tie That Binds." It's a reminder that being close to loved ones can be more important than material riches.

In 1772, after a few years in pastoral work, the Rev. John Fawcett, an English Baptist, was called to London to succeed the famous Dr. John Gill. His farewell sermon had been preached in his country church in Yorkshire. The wagons stood loaded with his furniture and books. All was ready for the family's departure.

But his loving congregation were heartbroken. Men, women, and children with sadness and tears gathered around the wagon. Others, sobbing, clung to him and his family.

Finally, overwhelmed with the sorrow of those they were leaving, Dr. Fawcett and his wife sat down on one of the packing cases and they, too, cried.

"Oh, John!" cried Mrs. Fawcett at last. "I cannot bear this! I know not how I can leave these dear friends. How will I be able to go?"

"Nor can I, either," replied her husband. "And we will not go. The wagons shall be unloaded, and everything returned to its old place."

The friends that had gathered were filled with intense joy and gratitude at this turn of events.

Dr. Fawcett at once sent a letter to London explaining their decision and then resolutely returned to his work on his pitifully small salary.

This hymn was written to commemorate the event. So universal are the sentiments it expresses that it has become one of our immortal hymns.

Blest Be the Tie That Binds

Friends and family members are often separated by distance. But we know that God is the tie that binds us all together, no matter where we are.

Blest be the tie that binds
Our hearts in Christian love;
The fellowship of kindred minds
Is like to that above.

Before our Father's throne
We pour our ardent pray'rs;
Our fears, our hopes, our aims are
   one—
Our comforts and our cares.

When we asunder part
It gives us inward pain,
But we shall still be joined in
   heart,
And hope to meet again.

REV. JOHN FAWCETT

Kindness Fills the Heart with Joy

We cannot tell the precise moment
when friendship is formed. As in
filling a vessel drop by drop, there
is at last a drop which makes it run
over, so in a series of kindnesses
there is at last one that makes the
heart run over.

SAMUEL JOHNSON

When friendships are real, they are not glass threads, or frostwork, but the solidest thing we know.

RALPH WALDO EMERSON

Go often to the house of thy friend, for weeds choke up the unused path.

SCANDINAVIAN EDDA

If you love someone you will be loyal to him no matter what the cost. You will always believe in him, always expect the best of him, and always stand your ground in defending him.

1 CORINTHIANS 13:7 LB

Oh, the comfort—the inexpressible comfort of feeling safe with a person—having neither to weigh thoughts nor measure words, but pouring them all right out, just as they are, chaff and grain together; certain that a faithful hand will take them and sift them, keep what is worth keeping, and then with the breath of kindness blow the rest away.

DINAH MARIA MULOCK CRAIK

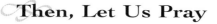

Then, Let Us Pray

*It's amazing, yet true, that often—at the
very time of our desperate need—God,
through the Holy Spirit, has led someone to
intercede on our behalf.*

The day was long, the burden I had borne
    Seemed heavier than I could longer
        bear;
And then it lifted—but I did not know
    Someone had knelt in prayer.

Had taken me to God that very hour,
    And asked the easing of the load, and He,
In infinite compassion, had stooped down
    And lifted the burden from me.

We cannot tell how often as we pray
    For some bewildered one, hurt and distressed,
The answer comes, but many times these hearts
    Find sudden peace and rest.

Someone had prayed, and faith, a lifted hand
    Reached up to God, and He reached down that day.
So many, many hearts have need of prayer—
    Then, let us, let us pray.

AUTHOR UNKNOWN

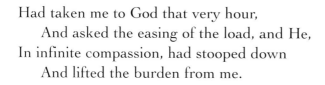

*To be a friend you must be there—
encouraging, cheering, empathizing, crying.
It's all part of the package of friendship.*

Pray for One Another

People can often sense when someone is in need of prayer—even if that someone is miles away. If the thought of a friend should come into your mind, why not stop to say a little prayer on their behalf?

I cannot tell why there should
    come to me
      A thought of someone miles
      and miles away,
In swift insistence on the memory,
      Unless a need there be that I
      should pray.

Too hurried oft are we to spare
    the thought
      For days together, of some
      friend away;
Perhaps God does it for us, and
    we ought
      To read this signal as a call to
      pray.

Perhaps, just then, my friend has
    fiercer fight
      And more appalling weakness,
      and decay
Of courage, darkness, some lost
    sense of right
      And so in case he needs my
      prayer, I pray.

Friend, do the same for me. If I
    intrude
      Unasked upon you, on some
      crowded day,
Give me a moment's prayer as
    interlude;
      Be very sure I need it;
      therefore pray.

MARIANNE FARNINGHAM

Friendship

Friendship—
a fleeting thing
that comes and goes.
What makes it last,
the magic ingredient?
Nobody knows!
Charisma, interest,
need, and caring,
human involvement,
loving, sharing,
a smile, a card,
friendship to see,
loving a person,
and letting them be,
remembering, talking,
baring your heart,
complex and simple
many things share a part.
Friendship is more than emotion.
Friendships are here to stay.
If we want to have more friends,
we must give more love away.

Love forgets mistakes; nagging about them parts the best of friends.

PROVERBS 17:9 LB

What a Friend Does

Experts have long known the value of friendships. The billion-dollar greet-ing card industry, as well as various poems, books, and songs, all extol the value of friendship.

A friend affirms the worth of another individual: by letting them know they are loved and appreciated just as they are; by not trying to lead them to make changes to fit into a particular mold, but allowing them to be unique; and by helping them discover their God-given talents and abilities and provid-ing opportunities where these gifts can be used and grow. It is with friends that we test our self-worth in the world.

Your best friend believes in you enough to enable you to go out and act upon your dreams and desires so that you are finally able to believe in yourself. Friendships help keep us healthy—physically, mentally, and spiritually. A friend does not always have all the answers, but will go with you to God to hear from Him.

Becoming a Friend

It takes work to be the helpful, considerate, caring person that others will want to know and spend time with, but it is well worth the investment.

Being a friend means that you need to reach out. Is there someone you can think of who needs to know that you are there for them—that you are a friend who cares? Pray for the spirit of friendship to light up your life so that you'll radiate this brightness to someone who needs you.

"Dear God, shine through me and help me lighten another's darkness by showing the same friendship that you extended. Show me a person that is in desperate need of a friend today. Help me to be sensitive, caring, and willing to go out of my way to meet this person's need right now, whether it be emotional, physical, or spiritual. Thank you that when I need a friend, YOU are 'the friend that sticketh closer than a brother.' In Jesus' name, Amen."

The stars come nightly to the sky;
The tidal wave unto the sea;
Nor time, nor space, nor deep, nor
    high
Can keep my own away from me.
Friendship is the triple alliance of
    the three great powers,
        Love, Sympathy, and Help.
My friends have come to me
    unsought; the great God
    gave them to me.

RALPH WALDO EMERSON

Service

To serve means to assist or be of use. Serving is one of the reasons we are on this earth and the reason Jesus Himself said He came to earth. When we serve, we reach out to meet the needs of others; service is an outward sign that we belong to God and desire to do His will. True service is not about grudgingly doing for others out of obligation but an act that flows willingly, as a channel for God's love. True servants give not just with their hands but with their hearts as well.

A Humble Servant

Jesus washed His disciples' feet as an example of how to be a servant.

Jesus knew that the time had come to leave this world to go to the Father. Having loved his dear companions, he continued to love them right to the end. It was suppertime. The Devil by now had Judas, son of Simon the Iscariot, firmly in his grip, all set for the betrayal.

Jesus knew that the Father had put him in complete charge of everything, that he came from God and was on his way back to God. So he got up from the supper table, set aside his robe, and put on an apron. Then he poured water into a basin and began to wash the feet of the disciples, drying them with an apron. When he got to Simon Peter, Peter said, "Master, you wash my feet?"

Jesus answered, "You don't understand now what I'm doing, but it will be clear enough to you later."

Peter persisted, "You're not going to wash my feet—ever!"

Jesus said, "If I don't wash you, you can't be part of what I'm doing."

"Master!" said Peter. "Not only my feet, then. Wash my hands! Wash my head!"

Jesus said, "If you've had a bath in the morning, you only need your feet washed now and you're clean from head to toe. My concern, you understand, is holiness, not hygiene. So now you're clean. But not every one of you." (He knew who was betraying him. That's why he said, "Not every one of you.") After he had finished washing their feet, he took his robe, put it back on, and went back to his place at the table.

Then he said, "Do you understand what I have done to you? You address me as 'Teacher' and 'Master' and rightly so. That is what I am. So if I, the Master and Teacher, washed your feet, you must now wash each other's feet. I've laid down a pattern for you. What I've done, you do. I'm only pointing out the obvious. A servant is not ranked above his master; an employee doesn't give orders to the employer. If you understand what I'm telling you, act like it—live a blessed life."

JOHN 13:4–17 THE MESSAGE

Ready for Service

Our strengths were given to us to help us serve. God rejoices when we change our "How can I help myself?" attitude to one of "How can I help other people?"

Strength is for service, not status. Each one of us needs to look after the good of the people around us, asking ourselves, "How can I help?"

That's exactly what Jesus did. He didn't make it easy for himself by avoiding people's troubles, but waded right in and helped out. "I took on the troubles of the troubled," is the way Scripture puts it.

ROMANS 15:2–3 THE MESSAGE

Desire Usefulness

The search for pleasure, wealth, and fame often leads to frustration. It seems the more we get, the more we want. To be useful is a goal that brings rewards far beyond earthly pleasures.

There are really only four great practical ends for which men and women can work in this world,—Pleasure, Wealth, Fame, and Useful- ness. We owe it to ourselves to consider them carefully, and to make up our minds which of them is to be our chief object in life...the one end that is really worth working for,—usefulness. To desire and strive to be of some service to the world, to aim at doing something which shall really increase the happiness and welfare and virtue of mankind—this is a choice which is possible for all of us; and surely it is a good haven to sail for....

   To have this for the chief aim in life ennobles and dignifies all that it touches. Wealth that comes as the reward of usefulness can be accepted with honour; and, consecrated to further usefulness, it becomes royal. Fame that comes from noble service, the gratitude of men, be they few or many, to one who has done them good, is true glory; and the influ- ence that it brings is as near to godlike power as anything that man can attain. But whether these temporal rewards are bestowed upon us or

not, the real desire of the soul is satis- fied just in being useful. The pleas- ant word that a man can hear at the close of the days, whispered in secret to his soul, is, "Well done, good and faithful servant!"

HENRY VAN DYKE,
COUNSELS BY THE WAY

Things Servants Say

The mark of a servant is willingness. We need to have an attitude of submitting to God's agenda rather than clinging to our own.

"What shall I do...?" Moses speaking. — Exodus 17:4 Amplified

"Speak, Lord, for Your servant is listening." Samuel speaking. — 1 Samuel 3:10 Amplified

"Here am I. Send me!" Isaiah speaking. — Isaiah 6:8 NASB

"Behold the maidservant of the Lord! Let it be to me according to your word." Mary speaking. — Luke 1:38 NKJV

"Not my will, but Thine be done." Jesus speaking. — Luke 22:42 NASB

"Lord, what wilt thou have me to do?" Paul speaking. — Acts 9:6 KJV

Anyone wanting to be the greatest must be the least—the servant of all.

MARK 9:35 LB

Receiving Service from Others

Those of us who consider ourselves the Lord's servants sometimes have a hard time receiving from others. Although Jesus said, "It's more blessed to give than receive," this statement also says, "It is blessed to receive."

While I was out for a couple hours,
my houseguests cleaned the house.
Instead of feeling grateful,
I felt hurt.
I know they were trying to help,
but I felt they were communicating,
"You are an inefficient housekeeper,
so we have to help you."
Why is it that I served them
the whole time they were here,
but when they tried to do a service
for me I couldn't handle it?
Didn't Jesus wash the apostles' feet?
I only want to wash other people's feet.
Lord, please humble me enough
to let them wash mine.

Love for God

Love for God is the best motive for serving.

If we are devoted to the cause of humanity, we shall soon be crushed and broken-hearted . . . but if our motive is love to God, no ingratitude can hinder us from serving our fellow men.

OSWALD CHAMBERS, *MY UTMOST FOR HIS HIGHEST*

Let Your Light Shine Through Serving

You are the light of the world. A city set on a hill cannot be hid. Nor do men light a lamp and put it under a peck-measure but on a lamp stand, and it gives light to all in the house. Let your light so shine before men that they may see your moral excellence and praiseworthy, noble and good deeds, and recognize and honor and praise and glorify your Father Who is in heaven.

MATTHEW 5:14–16 AMPLIFIED

Serving God and Others

What a mystery that when we serve others, it's as if we are doing the service for God!

One of the principal rules of religion is to lose no occasion of serving God. And since he is invisible to our eyes, we are to serve him in our neighbor, which he receives as if done to himself in person, standing visibly before us.

JOHN WESLEY

Jesus Explains Service to Others

If we serve others, we serve God. If we serve the "least," we serve Jesus because He came to earth to become one of the least.

"'...for I was hungry and you gave Me food; I was thirsty and you gave Me drink; I was a stranger and you took Me in;

'I was naked and you clothed Me; I was sick and you visited Me; I was in prison and you came to Me.'

"Then the righteous will answer Him, saying, 'Lord when did we see You hungry and feed You, or thirsty and give You drink?

'When did we see You a stranger and take You in, or naked and clothe You?

'Or when did we see You sick, or in prison and come to You?'

"And the King will answer and say to them, 'Assuredly, I say to you, inasmuch as you did it to one of the least of these My brethren, you did it to Me.'"

MATTHEW 25:35–40 NKJV

Serving with a Purpose

Work can be drudgery when we see it as just a job. Every area of work, no matter how insignificant it may seem, is an opportunity to faithfully serve God and people.

For our God never considers our work as merely a way to earn a living—so much an hour, so much a year. He has given each of us the gift of life with a specific purpose in view. To Him work is a sacrament, even what we consider unimportant, mundane work. When done "as unto the Lord," it can have eternal significance.

CATHERINE MARSHALL,
MEETING GOD AT EVERY TURN

A Full Life

Those with the fullest and most fulfilling lives are those who are busy serving others.

Life

Life is a gift to be used every day,
Not to be smothered and hidden away;
It isn't a thing to be stored in a chest
Where you gather your keepsakes and treasure your best;
It isn't a joy to be sipped now and then
And promptly put back in a dark place again.

Life is a gift that the humblest may boast of
And one that the humblest may well make the most of.
Get out and live it each hour of the day,
Wear it and use it as much as you may;
Don't keep it in niches and corners and grooves,
You'll find that in service its beauty improves.

EDGAR A. GUEST, *A HEAP O' LIVIN'*

Serving the Dying

Many people have found comfort through hospice care—both the terminally ill patients and their loved ones. Even the nurses, doctors, and volunteers who provide hospice care often find their own lives changed in the process.

A friend who didn't drive asked if I could take her to the Hospice volunteer–training classes she was attending. My first reaction was to think of the discomfort I felt around dying people, even though I'd been a nurse years before—their suffering unnerved me. But I decided to take the classes with her, just to see what it was all about. Soon I discovered there were ways to ease my discomfort around dying people, but even more importantly, there were ways I could help ease their suffering. The main thing I saw in the volunteers and workers who helped us in the training was that they cared so much about people—I wanted to care that much, too.

At first it seemed painfully difficult to go into a stranger's room at the Hospice house where I've volunteered for the past 1½ years. I would plead to God: "Show me what to do and say!" And He has.

I've learned many things from serving as a Hospice volunteer. I've learned about dying with dignity and releasing one's suffering to God. I've learned how to be a better listener. I've learned how important it is to "seize the day," and even the moment—there are times I would say to myself, "I'll stop in and see her next time," and the next time wouldn't come because she had died. I've learned that even the little things matter—like a smile, a hug, holding someone's hand, reading from the Bible, or pushing a patient outside in a wheelchair.

I've learned about the power of prayer. One time a patient said, "I can't handle this anymore." I knew she believed in God, so I asked, "Do you want me to pray for you?" She said yes, so I did—out loud. God gave her peace and strength to make it over that hurdle.

I've learned that dying time can be a beautiful time, despite the suffering and uncertainty involved. I've learned how to mourn with those who mourn. I've learned about dealing with my own grief and loss and how to let go of self-pity, so I can cherish the act of living my life.

Serving with Hospice has given me an education no textbook could provide. And it has changed me—for the better.

A HOSPICE VOLUNTEER

The wonder of serving is when we meet the needs of others, forgetting about our own, and yet somehow in the process our needs are met.

Serving God because you are God's friend puts a permanent end to duty.

EUGENIA PRICE, *WHAT REALLY MATTERS*

Serving in the Struggle for Freedom

Martin Luther King, Jr., had a dream that people of all races could be lifted from oppression. He dedicated his life to the service of the black community in order to fulfill that dream.

What if he had died, he asked the audience, when he was stabbed in 1958 in Harlem? He would have missed the greatest experience of his life in the freedom struggle of the black people. There were difficult days ahead, he said, days of confusion and doubt to live through. He was not discouraged by this, on the contrary. "It really doesn't matter with me now. Because I've been to the mountaintop.... I've looked over and I've seen the Promised Land." Then he gave the people whom he had served so well his final promise, and his prophesy. "I may not get there with you," he said, "but I want you to know tonight, that we as a people will get to the Promised Land. So I'm happy tonight. I'm not worried about anything. I'm not fearing any man."

LILLIE PATTERSON, *MARTIN LUTHER KING, JR., AND THE FREEDOM MOVEMENT*

On Being a Servant

Each of us is called to a life of service. God's voice may sound in our own inner conversations, in encouraging a friend, in hearing a specific need, or in realizing that we have specific skills that could help others. How is God calling you to serve?

I don't know what your destiny will be, but one thing I do know: the only ones among you who will be really happy are those who have sought and found how to serve.

ALBERT SCHWEITZER

Whatever your task, work heartily, as serving the Lord and not men, knowing that from the Lord you will receive the inheritance as your reward; you are serving the Lord Christ.

COLOSSIANS 3:23–24 RSV

One Group of Faithful Servants

Teaching can be a thankless job with low pay and public criticism. Teach-ers' servant hearts keep them going. Parents need to thank their children's teachers for their service.

Some of the greatest servants
I know are teachers.
They don't get paid much,
but they give much.
So many go the extra mile
to encourage my child.
To say, "You can do it—
I know you can."
They see beyond
the outer shell
to what's inside,
and they minister
to the heart
while trying to
teach the brain
to think.

They endure the criticism
of parents
and administration
and the press
and professional critics.
And still they serve on.
Rarely does a student say,
"Thank you for being
such a great teacher."
Often, we don't even think
of it until years later,
when we realize the impact
a teacher has made on our lives.
And so I thank you, teachers,
one and all
for being such faithful servants.

*All the service
that weighs an ounce
in the sight of God
is that which is
prompted by love.*

BILLY SUNDAY, *THE REAL BILLY SUNDAY*

A Grateful Servant

A dedicated servant is grateful to all those who have served him, including the Lord. He sees that he is passing on to others what he has received.

As we drove home, I thought about how blessed I've been. I've received many honors and awards and much attention since accepting the Crystal Apple from President Reagan, but I realized that no award was greater than knowing Jesus Christ.

Not only had Jesus given me Himself, but He also had blessed me with a beautiful wife and children. Jesus had shown me love through common people — people who had molded and shaped my dreams, even when they didn't know they were teaching me.

GUY DOUD, *MOLDER OF DREAMS*

Seeing Beyond the Dirt

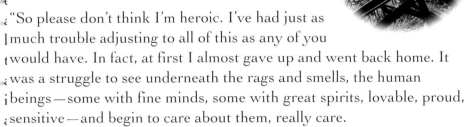

Seeing beyond the "dirt" to the beauty and goodness of those we serve is essential. We can do it if we look at them through the eyes of the Lord. This is seen in the following example, which the author based on her mother's experience teaching poor Appalachian children.

"So please don't think I'm heroic. I've had just as much trouble adjusting to all of this as any of you would have. In fact, at first I almost gave up and went back home. It was a struggle to see underneath the rags and smells, the human beings — some with fine minds, some with great spirits, lovable, proud, sensitive — and begin to care about them, really care.

"It's like — well, like garden vegetables. If you threw out your turnips because they came out of the ground with dirt clinging to them, you'd never discover the goodness there."

CATHERINE MARSHALL, *CHRISTY*

A Servant Reflects

Billy Graham has served the Lord faithfully for decades since he began preaching in 1938. Yet he sees where he could have done better—a sign of a truly humble servant.

Although I have much to be grateful for as I look back over my life, I also have many regrets. I have failed many times, and I would do many things differently.

For one thing, I would speak less and study more, and I would spend more time with my family. When I look back over the schedule I kept thirty or forty years ago, I am staggered by all the things we did and the engagements we kept. Sometimes we flitted from one part of the country to another, even from one continent to another, in the course of only a few days. Were all those engagements necessary? Was I as discerning as I might have been about which ones to take and which to turn down? I doubt it. Every day I was absent from my family is gone forever.

BILLY GRAHAM, *JUST AS I AM*

All service ranks the same with God.

ROBERT BROWNING

Serve the Lord with gladness . . .

PSALM 100:2 NASB

Rewards of Serving

There's a fulfilling joy that comes from serving other people rather than putting our own desires first.

Rosalynn and I enjoy vacations, and we could go to Hawaii or on a Caribbean cruise every summer for about the same amount it costs us to travel to one of the Habitat building sites. But when I look back on the last twelve years or so, I see that some of my most memorable and gratifying experiences were when I joined other volunteers and worked to exhaustion building a house alongside the family who would live there.

JIMMY CARTER, *LIVING FAITH*

Benefits from Service

If we look to service for the benefits it will bring us, we may be disappointed. Yet, if we forget about the benefits and gladly serve others, good things happen to us. We are helped in so many ways by those we serve.

We are here taught the great lessons, that to get, we must give; that to accumulate, we must scatter; that to make ourselves happy, we must make others happy; and that in order to become spiritually vigorous, we must seek the spiritual good of others. In watering others, we are ourselves watered. How? Our efforts to be useful *bring out our powers for usefulness*. We have latent talents and dormant faculties, which are brought to light by exercise. Our strength for labor is hidden even from ourselves, until we venture forth to fight the Lord's battles, or to climb the mountains of difficulty. We do not know what tender sympathies we possess, until we try to dry the widow's tears, and soothe the orphan's grief. We often find, in attempting to teach others, that we *gain instruction for ourselves*. Oh, what gracious lessons some of us have learned at sick beds! We went to teach the Scriptures; we came away blushing that we knew so little of them. In our converse with poor saints, we are taught the way of God more perfectly for ourselves, and get a deeper insight into divine truth. So that watering others *makes us humble*. We discover how much grace there is where we had not looked for it, and how much the poor saint may outstrip us in knowledge. Our own *comfort is always increased* by our working for others. We endeavor to cheer them, and the consolation gladdens our own heart. Like the two men in the snow: one chafed the other's limbs to keep him from dying, and in so doing kept his own blood in circulation, and saved his own life.

CHARLES SPURGEON, *MORNING BY MORNING*

Perseverance

There are many events in our lives over which we have no control. However, we do have a choice either to endure trying times and press on or to give up. The secret of survival, whether or not we question God's presence or His ability to help us, is remembering that our hope is in the fairness, goodness, and justice of God. When we put our trust in the character of a God who cannot fail us, we will remain faithful. Our trust and faithfulness produce the endurance that sees us through the "tough stuff" we all face in this life.

Don't Quit

For several decades, this famous poem has hung on refrigerators in homes across America and has been mailed to discouraged college students by their parents.

When things go wrong, as they sometimes will,
When the road you're trudging seems all up hill,
When the funds are low and the debts are high,
And you want to smile, but you have to sigh,
When care is pressing you down a bit,
Rest, if you must—but don't you quit.

Life is queer with its twists and turns,
As every one of us sometimes learns,
And many a failure turns about
When he might have won had he stuck it out;
Don't give up, though the pace seems slow—
You might succeed with another blow.
Often the goal is nearer than
It seems to a faint and faltering man,
Often the struggler has given up
When he might have captured the victor's cup.
And he learned too late, when the night
    slipped down,
How close he was to the golden crown.

Success is failure turned inside out—
The silver tint of the clouds of doubt—
And you never can tell how close you are,
It may be near when it seems afar;
So stick to the fight when you're hardest hit—
It's when things seem worst that you must not quit.

CLINTON HOWELL

The Broken String

We often face tasks that seem to have insurmountable odds. But if we make the most of whatever we have, the results are guaranteed to be beautiful.

Paganini, the world-famed violinist, was once playing before an audience when, in the midst of his brilliant performance, a string snapped. He played on, only to have a second fail him. With but two strings he continued his rendition. Then a third broke. With but one string at his command the master-player, unfaltering and undismayed, proceeded to the end with such brilliance and skill that his audience burst into a frenzy of applause. Paganini was but a man; our master-player is God. We may seem to ourselves to be of little use, dull and unresponsive, gifted with but a single string, yet if the instrument of our lives be wholly given up to Him, He will use it to bring forth heavenly glory under the power and skill of his touch.

Norman B. Harrison,
His Very Own

Great works are performed not by strength but by perseverance.

Samuel Johnson

Sometimes It Means Beginning Again

There are times when we are forced to do a laborious task—and then do it all over again. But if we follow it through to the end, the results can be better than we ever expected. The following story about author Thomas Carlyle is an excellent example.

We all have dreams of what we want to achieve during our lifetime. But few "endure to the end" to see their God-given dreams become realities. To achieve our dreams we must first set a long-range goal and objective. For many this is difficult because of vague ideas about what they might want to do "sometime." Without specific goals, nothing significant can happen.

After we have set our objective, we must think about the specific steps we can take to reach this goal. As we take each step, we are making a commitment to press on. The only thing that helps us at this stage is perseverance. Perseverance makes it possible for us to believe that we can accomplish what we've set out to.

Thomas Carlyle had finished writing his tremendous manuscript, *History of the French Revolution.* He gave it to his neighbor, John Stuart Mill, to read. Several days later Mill came to Carlyle's home, pale and nervous, to report to Carlyle that his maid had used the manuscript to start a fire!

Carlyle was in a frenzy for days. Two years of labor lost. He could never muster the energy to write again. A task that large was overwhelming the first time. The thought of having to write the whole thing over was almost paralyzing.

One day, as Carlyle was walking the streets, he saw a stonemason building a long, high wall. He stood watching for a long time before he was suddenly impressed with the fact that the wall was being built one brick at a time! He took inspiration from that experience and decided, "I'll just write one page today, and then one page tomorrow. One page at a time, that's all I'll think about."

He started small and slow. The task was tedious, but he stayed with it and went on to finish the work. The end result was better than the first time!

Don't let bad memories or unfortunate incidents move in and dominate you. You won't get very far by looking in the rearview mirror—you must look ahead! Perseverance enables you to live in such a way that you can *make* good things happen.

Provoke One Another

There's an often misunderstood verse in the Bible: "And let us consider one another to provoke unto love and to good works" (Hebrews 10:24 KJV).

In this context, the above verse means that we are to arouse, incite, hearten. What a wonderful character quality: to be able to awaken and inspire others to live righteously and godly in this present world.

We don't often think about how much failure is simply due to the lack of incentive or courage or loss of spirit. When we "lose heart" in our projects, there is no longer any vision to propel us toward our goals. This is when we can become cheerleaders to our struggling friends. This is how we hearten and provoke others to good works.

The Spur to Untiring Service

When we remember that we are working for the rewards of heaven and not for the praise of people, we are able to press on and persevere in the tasks ahead of us.

How much this teaching is needed in a day of superficial and man-made methods to maintain good works in the face of flagging energies.... How many dear people of God are fainting in their service because men are slow to approve or slightly applaud. Stung to inaction by the sense of ingratitude! We all need to turn often to these Scriptures to nerve us to renewed service. Men require a sense of reward, somehow, somewhere. We have it, fully assured, from Him and in Him. Beyond all that He may give us will be Himself. Anticipating the sight of His face then, we need to see Him now, as the antidote to faintness and weariness, the sufficient spur to untiring service.

NORMAN B. HARRISON, *HIS VERY OWN*

Keep up the good work and don't get discouraged, for you will be rewarded.

2 CHRONICLES 15:7 LB

Have courage for the great sorrows of life and patience for the small ones; and when you have laboriously accomplished your daily task, go to sleep in peace. God is awake.

VICTOR HUGO

Gratitude for Work

Thank God every morning when you get up that you have something to do which must be done, whether you like it or not. Being forced to work, and forced to do your best, will breed in you temperance and self-control, diligence and strength of will, cheerfulness and content, and a hundred virtues which the idle never know.

CHARLES KINGSLEY

Because the Lord God helps me, I will not be dismayed; therefore, I have set my face like flint to do his will, and I know that I will triumph.

ISAIAH 50:7 LB

Keep on Working

Though I walk in the midst of trouble, thou dost preserve my life; thou dost stretch out thy hand against the wrath of my enemies, and thy right hand delivers me. The Lord will fulfil his purpose for me; thy steadfast love, O Lord, endures for ever. Do not forsake the work of thy hands.

PSALM 138:7–8 RSV

And let us not be weary in well doing: for in due season we shall reap, if we faint not.

GALATIANS 6:9 KJV

Perseverance

When You Feel Defeated

Too many of us let the little things in life defeat us. But many outstanding figures in history have had to overcome obstacles before they became successful—perhaps that is part of what made them so great.

There is a man who once lived in America who inspires all of us, yet this man knew the meaning of defeat. His mother died when he was a child. As a young man, he ran for the legislature of his state, but he was defeated.

He entered business, but a worthless partner put him into bankruptcy. He fell passionately in love with a girl, but she died.

He served one term in Congress, but was defeated for re-election. He tried for an appointment to the United States Land Office, but failed to get it. He tried to be a lyceum lecturer, but he failed in that also.

He ran for the United States Senate, but was defeated. He ran for vice-president of the United States, but was defeated.

His name was Abraham Lincoln.

CHARLES L. ALLEN, *WHEN YOU GRADUATE*

Try, Try Again

Many parents have quoted this favorite old poem to their children. The lesson may be simple, but it's an important one to learn!

'Tis a lesson you should heed,
    Try, try again;
If at first you don't succeed,
    Try, try again;
Then your courage should appear,
For, if you will persevere,
You will conquer, never fear;
    Try, try again.

Once or twice though you should
    fail,
    Try, try again;
If you would at last prevail,
    Try, try again;
If we strive, 'tis no disgrace
Though we do not win the race;
What should you do in this case?
    Try, try again.

Time will bring you your reward,
    Try, try again.
All that other folks can do,
Why, with patience, should not
    you?
Only keep this rule in view;
    Try, try again.

W. E. HICKSON

Water, Wind, and Faith

Jesus challenges us to have faith in God even in the midst of the windstorms of our lives.

Even when there is no water around, we know what it is like to be in that boat. We even use similar language. We have "stormy" days, "stormy" relationships. We are "swamped" by all the work we have to do. We feel the list growing of things to do. We see the

approaching deadlines. We know the pressure to achieve much and accomplish more. When we add the family calendar, the relatives, and the needs of the world, our boat often seems ready to capsize.

Sometimes it feels like there is no way out. The problems threaten to dump us into the sea, and we cannot see how we are going to make it.

At such times we cry out, "Help!" We want Jesus, or someone, to save us. Scripture is full of such cries. "Save me, O God, for the waters have come up to my neck" (Psalm 69:1 NRSV). We are in good company when we cry out to God.

Our challange is to trust that not only does God hear our cry, but that He is also working in the very midst of our windstorm. Jesus is revealing to the disciples and to us a God who cares for the well-being of all people, especially those feeling swamped.

We need not worry how God will calm the storms, only that He will. Each storm calmed leads us to greater trust, a deeper faith. God can help us deal with the constant pressures of our days. God can bring calm to our stormy lives.

A windstorm arose on the sea, so great that the boat was being swamped by the waves; but he was asleep. And they went and woke him up, saying, "Lord, save us! We are perishing!" And he said to them, "Why are you afraid, you of little faith?" Then he got up and rebuked the winds and the sea; and there was a dead calm. They were amazed.

MATTHEW 8:24–27 NRSV

"Come to Me, all you who labor and are heavy-laden and over-burdened, and I will cause you to rest—I will ease and relieve and refresh your souls. Take My yoke upon you, and learn of Me; for I am gentle (meek) and humble (lowly) in heart, and you will find rest—relief, ease and refreshment and recreation and blessed quiet—for your souls. For My yoke is wholesome (useful, good)—not harsh, hard, sharp or pressing, but comfortable, gracious and pleasant; and My burden is light and easy to be borne."

MATTHEW 11:28–30 AMPLIFIED

Commit everything you do to the Lord.
Trust him to help you do it and he will.

PSALM 37:5 LB

Perseverance

Blessed Assurance

*This popular hymn may best be
remembered as the theme song that
George Beverly Shea led the choir
and congregation in singing at
every Billy Graham evangelistic
crusade.*

Blessed assurance, Jesus is mine!
Oh what a foretaste of glory
    divine!
Heir of salvation, purchase of God,
Born of His Spirit, washed in His
    blood.

Perfect submission, perfect delight!
Visions of rapture now burst on my sight;
Angels descending bring from above
Echoes of mercy, whispers of love.

Perfect submission—all is at rest,
I in my Savior am happy and blest;
Watching and waiting, looking above,
Filled with His goodness, lost in His love.

Chorus:
This is my story, this is my song,
Praising my Savior all the day long;
This is my story, this is my song,
Praising my Savior all the day long.

FANNY J. CROSBY

Stand by Your Work

The following excerpt is from the Letter to Teachers that C. E. Leslie wrote in the front of his often-used music textbook. In it, he reminds us that teaching and music are two of life's greatest pursuits, and that no matter what our profession is, we should always perform with our best efforts, creativity, and the highest enthusiasm.

Dear Teacher,

Your success greatly depends on your own efforts; you must be intensely interested in your profession.

Do not devote all your time to the study of music, but to the study of development; of how best to teach your pupils to comprehend it. The successful teacher is the one who can, in the most simple way, and in the shortest space of time, teach his pupils to understand the subject under consideration.

Do not confine yourself to text books; be original; use the blackboard, make your exercises short and to the point. Do not dwell too long on one subject; keep your pupils interested. After you have taught them to read music, have them frequently study silent singing. Silent singing is *thought getting.* Oral singing is the *giving of the thought* from the printed page, and we must have the thought before we can give it to others.

Teacher, again let me urge you to be honest and faithful in the profession you have chosen. Stand by the work twelve months in the year. Separation means loss of power. You may be doing only rudimental work, but if honestly and well done, it will meet with God's approval.

Music is one of God's greatest gifts to man. Electric wires, railroads and steamships

make the whole world as one city; but the vibrations of music produce the only electric current that binds earth to heaven. When you are singing, "O for a closer walk with God!" it may be rudimental work, but it is the only power you can call upon for relief, or that will satisfy your weary heart. When you sing, "I know that my Redeemer Liveth," it may be the echo as it comes back to us from that heavenly shore: "Peace, peace, peace to thy weary soul!" Rudimental work is the foundation upon which all of our lives are builded. Be not ashamed of your position. When a great General falls in battle his life and heroic deeds are heralded to all the world upon the pages of history. The private soldier who shouldered his musket, bade his loved ones goodby, and went to his death in defense of his country, fills perhaps an unknown grave; but in God's book of memory his name is registered, and the angels have written opposite, the word Hero. It is not the position that tells, but the earnest and conscientious discharge of the duties belonging to it. Be faithful in the work entrusted to your care.

Teacher, if I can help you on to success, let me know it. I am your friend, use me as such.

Yours, very truly, C. E. Leslie

C. E. LESLIE, *LESLIE'S CROWN OF SONG*

God, you're leading me.
With confidence I face my day.
Every duty and interruption
are appointments
you've sent my way.

But thanks be to God, who gives us the victory through our Lord Jesus Christ. Therefore, my beloved brethren, be steadfast, immovable, always abounding in the work of the Lord, knowing that in the Lord your labor is not in vain.

1 CORINTHIANS 15:57–58 RSV

He that overcometh shall inherit all things; and I will be his God, and he shall be my son.

REVELATION 21:7 KJV

O God, Our Help in Ages Past

This old hymn of the church is taken from the words of Psalm 90.

O God, our help in ages past,
    Our hope for years to
    come,
Our shelter from the stormy blast,
    And our eternal home!

Under the shadow of Thy throne,
    Still may we dwell secure;
Sufficient is Thine arm alone,
    And our defense is sure.

Before the hills in order stood,
    Or earth received her
    frame,
From everlasting Thou art God,
    To endless years the same.

A thousand ages, in Thy sight,
    Are like an evening gone;
Short as the watch that ends the
    night,
    Before the rising sun.

O God, our help in ages past,
    Our hope for years to come,
Be Thou our guide while life shall
    last,
    And our eternal home.

ISAAC WATTS

A Psalm of Life

This poem reminds us that as we journey through life we can leave "footprints on the sands of time" for those who follow behind us.

Tell me not, in mournful numbers,
  Life is but an empty dream!
For the soul is dead that
    slumbers,
  And things are not what they
    seem.

Life is real! Life is earnest!
  And the grave is not its goal;
Dust thou art, to dust returnest,
  Was not spoken of the soul.

Not enjoyment, and not sorrow,
  Is our destined end or way;
But to act, that each to-morrow
  Finds us farther than to-day.

Art is long, and Time is fleeting,
  And our hearts, though stout
    and brave,
Still, like muffled drums, are
    beating
  Funeral marches to the grave.

In the world's broad field of
    battle,
  In the bivouac of Life,
Be not like dumb, driven cattle!
  Be a hero in the strife!

Trust no Future, howe'er
    pleasant!
  Let the dead Past bury its
    dead!
Act—act in the living Present!
  Heart within, and God
    o'erhead!

Lives of great men all remind us,
  We can make our lives
    sublime,
And departing, leave behind us
  Footprints on the sands of
    time;

Footprints, that perhaps another,
  Sailing o'er life's solemn main,
A forlorn and shipwrecked
    brother,
  Seeing, shall take heart again.

Let us, then, be up and doing,
  With a heart for any fate;
Still achieving, still pursuing,
  Learn to labour and to wait.

HENRY WADSWORTH LONGFELLOW

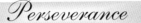

Perseverance

Perseverance Means More Than Endurance

God will not delay a minute longer than necessary to bring us the direction, answers, and relief we seek and pray for.

Perseverance means more than endurance—more than simply holding on until the end. A saint's life is in the hands of God like a bow and arrow in the hands of an archer. God is aiming at something the saint cannot see, but our Lord continues to stretch and strain, and every once in a while the saint says, "I can't take any more." Yet God pays no attention; He goes on stretching until His purpose is in sight, and then He lets the arrow fly. Entrust yourself to God's hands. Is there something in your life for which you need perseverance right now? Maintain your intimate relationship with Jesus Christ through perseverance of faith.

OSWALD CHAMBERS, *MY UTMOST FOR HIS HIGHEST*

Failure: A Detour to Success

It has been observed that the only people who don't fail very much are those who don't try very much. Does that point also hold true with faith?

Simon had been at the top of the class among Jesus' prized pupils. And he was also the natural leader among the apostles. He had even been given the affectionate nickname Peter (meaning "Rock" or "Rocky") by Jesus, implying a key foundational role Simon would play for the church in the time ahead.

Unfortunately, things didn't continue in that direction for Simon Peter. Jesus eventually had to tell his closest followers what was on the horizon for him on their trip to Jerusalem. In keeping with God's plan, Jesus would have to suffer at the hands of the Jewish authorities and be sentenced to die on a Roman cross, before being raised from the dead.

This did not set well with Simon Peter. It ran contrary to his personal plans for Jesus. As a result, strong-willed Peter even went so far as to take Jesus aside and rebuke him. This was the first time Jesus had to warn Peter that he was unconsciously playing into Satan's hands with such short-sighted thinking.

What a shock that must have been to Peter! To be told by the Master that the Devil was using your deep concern would be highly confusing, to say the least. Perhaps it was even a little disillusioning, sowing a small seed of doubt in Peter's mind.

Then, after Jesus and the apostles arrived in Jerusalem, the warning was repeated, and at a very ironic point. The issue came up immediately after Jesus had spoken of the faithfulness of the apostles in trials. He promised them close fellowship and the authority to rule under him in the coming kingdom of God.

So far, so good! This was indeed music to Peter's ears. But Jesus then struck a sour note. He brought up Satan's eagerness to sift the lives of the apostles like so many kernels of grain. Most troubling of all was that Jesus focused this point at Simon Peter. Jesus pointed his finger at Peter, clearly implying that, although Satan desired to trouble the lives of all the apostles, he was particularly intent on getting to Peter.

But Jesus didn't stop there. Although he knew there would be a short-term failure of faith on the part of Peter and the other apostles, Jesus would not allow this to be long-term or permanent. He had prayed to the Father to enable Peter to get beyond that painful failure and to help restore and build up others in the Lord.

Jesus saw it coming, and he once again alerted Peter to the grave danger. But Peter wouldn't listen. He objected to Jesus' assertion, this time indicating that he had at least heard what Jesus had previously taught about his coming mistreatment and death in Jerusalem. He pledged allegiance to Jesus. He claimed to be willing to go to prison for Jesus, or even to die.

But Jesus knew that would not happen, at least not immediately (though Peter would be imprisoned more than once and would eventually die for Jesus). So Jesus indicated just how close at hand the danger to his faith was. Simon Peter would deny even knowing Jesus three times before the rooster crowed the next morning.

It is easy to visualize Peter's mouth, gaping open after Jesus'

words. It is also easy to read Peter's thoughts: That will never happen to me!

But it did happen. Peter and the remaining apostles broke and ran, when Jesus was arrested. That was bad enough! Then, the other apostles hid when Peter followed Jesus after his arrest. In the dark and chilly predawn hours, Simon Peter's faith failed repeatedly. He did, in fact, deny Jesus three times.

Fortunately, that was not the end! Though totally humiliated by his failure of faith, and quite hesitant to recommit himself (for fear of a like failure!), Peter was restored and proved to be even more effective in service for Jesus.

And let us not get tired of doing what is right, for after a while we will reap a harvest of blessing if we don't get discouraged and give up.

GALATIANS 6:9 LB

Perseverance is possible as long as we remain convinced that God is at work—changing people, changing our circumstances, and changing us.

Persevere in Obedience

"What is faith? It is the confident assurance that something we want is going to happen. It is the certainty that what we hope for is waiting for us, even though we cannot see it up ahead" (Hebrews 11:1 LB).

A problem
and a promise—
God has not left us
unarmed.
He has made a way of escape;
He will not have us
harmed.
Persevere in obedience—
He may be testing
your faith.
But He will lead you
victoriously
to arrive at
your
promised place.

Better is the end of a thing than the beginning thereof: and the patient in spirit is better than the proud in spirit.

Ecclesiastes 7:8 KJV

Trusting God's Promises

God may throw us a few curves in life—we may feel hassled, troubled, anxious, or uncomfortable, and not understand why our circumstances don't fit our desires. But if we trust in the wisdom of His plan, God will provide for all our needs.

It was November 1978. My husband, Bob, bounced through the front door of our Boise, Idaho, home calling, "Hi Honey! How was your day?"

An ominous feeling crept over me. I replied guardedly, "Oh, it was OK. How about yours?"

"Super. Today I was promoted, and we're moving back to Helena."

My mouth dropped open. I managed a muted "Oh! When?" We'd moved six times in the past 15 years, to Texas, California, Montana, Alaska, Washington, D.C., and Idaho. Montana had been my least favorite place.

Why had God regarded my husband's prayers more than my own? I asked Him, "God, do you know what you're doing? Why do we need to be uprooted now? How will we ever be able to sell our home or get the money to buy a new one? The market is so tight right now, and no one buys and sells houses at Christmastime. It'll never work."

God gets my attention best when I'm in His Word, so I flipped open my Bible. I read, *"Look! I'm living here in a cedar-paneled home. . . . Carry out your plan in every detail, for it is the will of the Lord. . . . And I have been with you everywhere you've gone"* (1 Chronicles 17:1–2, 8 LB).

Our house sold the first week it was on the market. We made it through sorting, packing, farewell parties, and moving—though we didn't yet have a new house to move into. Helena became a test in perseverance. I dreaded the daily trudging through snowdrifts in 20-degree weather to house-hunt. My fear of getting stuck in a snowbank became a reality several times. I wanted to go back inside, dive under the covers, and spend the day watching TV. But living in a motel was so depressing. We had to find a house *soon*!

I looked at ten houses a day for ten days, and nothing seemed right for us. I'd definitely not found the new cedar-paneled home I had expected since God spoke to me through his Word. "God, am I

wrong? Was I reading more into that Scripture than what you intended? Where do you want us to live? Where shall I look today? I don't even know which way to turn anymore. Help me please," I cried out as I stared at my coffee cup in the coffee shop.

My dejection turned to despair when the realtor arrived to show me today's "picks." When we arrived at the first house, he discovered the lockbox had been removed from the door, so we couldn't even get in! I remained in the car wondering about the futility of this trip, then turned to look at beautiful Mt. Helena rising a block to the north. This was definitely the location that we would prefer.

Then I saw a home being built across the street. "Can we go across the street and see the one under construction?"

His negative answer, "It's not one of my listings," didn't dampen my spirits.

"Then please, sir, take me back to my car. I must see that house. It's 'For Sale by Builder.'"

It took me less than 15 minutes to return to the home on the hill. My feet flew up the steps, "Is anyone here?"

A young man approached. "How can I help you?"

"Could you tell me what kind of wood is on the outside of this house? And on the fireplace wall?" My first questions no doubt sounded a little strange to the small cluster of men I'd just noticed working in the corner.

"Why, it's all cedar paneling," the builder answered.

"Is the house still for sale?" I asked breathlessly.

"Yes. Although that group of realtors just came to list it," he replied motioning to the window.

"Oh, please hold it for me. I know it's the one that God has chosen for us. I will call and ask my husband to come from work."

My husband's reply was, "If it's the house God has for us, then go ahead and buy it!"

I managed to restrain myself for 30 minutes until he arrived from his office. But there was never a doubt. God had done more than I could ask or think. Why had I ever doubted that I could trust Him with every detail of my life? As I wrote out our deposit check, I breathed a silent prayer, "God, thank you for once again showing how greatly you care for every detail of our lives."

God's Arms

Problems are a fact of life. Luckily, God is with us through them. He will help us persevere.

Lord, when we have nothing left to hold on to, you provide us with hope as an anchor for our souls. We need that hope now, and we pray that you will fill every broken place in our hearts with its reassuring light. Thank you, Lord, for in you we have an unending supply of hope in the midst of uncertainty and failure. We know that if we could see this situation through your eyes, we would see how you will bring us through it. Amen.

Hope in God

When everything seems hopeless, turning to God can make life seem worthwhile.

So many people walk through this life completely void of hope. There is no light in their eyes. They are so beaten down by life that they can barely get out of bed in the morning, let alone face the day with a bounce in their step. The Lord will touch these lost souls, these weary hearts, with the glorious truth of His love for them. He will give them that blessed assurance, that hope, that only comes from trusting in God. For such is the hope that makes all their days worth living.

God's Light Shows Hope

Held up to your light, our broken hearts can become prisms that scatter micro-rainbows on the wall. Our pain is useless as it is, redeeming God, just as a prism is a useless chunk of glass until light passes through it. Remind us that the smallest ray of sun in a shower can create a rainbow. Use our tears as the showers and your love as the sun. Looking up, we see the tiniest arches of hope in the lightening sky.

God Will Sustain Me

God, Himself, has said, "I will not in any way fail you, nor give you up, nor leave you without support. I will not, I will not, I will not, in any degree leave you helpless, nor forsake nor let you down" (Hebrews 13:5 Amplified).

People may fail me, friends seem to forsake me, and my family may act like they either don't care or don't understand. It is easy to become discouraged and tempting to give up when I look around at my circumstances.

But I will persevere—claiming the promise that God will not abandon me or fail me (Joshua 1:5). With the apostle of old I will confidently say, "The Lord is my Helper, I will not be seized with alarm—I will not fear or dread or be terrified. What can man do to me?" (Hebrews 13:6 Amplified).

Praying for Strength

O God . . . Help me to link my littleness to Thy greatness, my faintheartedness to Thy loving aggression, my holding back to Thy ongoingness, my fear to Thy faith—then nothing can stop me. Amen.

E. STANLEY JONES, *ABUNDANT LIVING*

Wisdom

The Bible urges us to "Acquire wisdom! Acquire understanding!" (Proverbs 4:5). We are instructed to have two goals: wisdom—knowing and doing right—and common sense. Wisdom is the ability to meet each situation with discernment and good judgment, whether in dealing with others, making choices, or dispensing justice. Wisdom involves using the knowledge we have to take the proper course of action—if we know and don't act, it is the same as not knowing at all. When we let Christ become the source of our wisdom, He will guide us in making wise decisions and acting on them.

Wisdom

Wisdom is more precious than rubies; nothing you desire can compare with her. PROVERBS 3:15 NLT

The Beginning of Wisdom

When we really want to acquire wisdom, we must start by getting to know God better.

Teach the wise, and they will be wiser. Teach the righteous, and they will learn more. Fear of the Lord is the beginning of wisdom. Knowledge of the Holy One results in understanding. Wisdom will multiply your days and add years to your life. If you become wise, you will be the one to benefit. If you scorn wisdom, you will be the one to suffer.

PROVERBS 9:9–12 NLT

Wisdom

To Be Counted Wise

To be known as a wise person, it's important to use your knowledge well and not flaunt it.

Do you want to be counted wise, to build a reputation for wisdom?
Here's what you do: Live well, live wisely, live humbly.
It's the way you live, not the way you talk, that counts.
Mean-spirited ambition isn't wisdom.
Boasting that you are wise isn't wisdom.
Twisting the truth to make yourselves sound wise isn't wisdom.
It's the furthest thing from wisdom—it's animal cunning, devilish
     conniving.
Whenever you're trying to look better than others or get the better of
     others,
things fall apart and everyone ends up at the others' throats.

Real wisdom, God's wisdom, begins with a holy life and is
characterized by getting along with others.
It is gentle and reasonable, overflowing with mercy and blessings,
not hot one day and cold the next, not two-faced.
You can develop a healthy, robust community that lives right with God
and enjoy its results *only* if you do the hard work of getting along with
each other, treating each other with dignity and honor.

JAMES 3:13–18 THE MESSAGE

275

Wisdom

Wisdom and Understanding

And the Spirit of the Lord will rest on him—the Spirit of wisdom and understanding, the Spirit of counsel and might, the Spirit of knowledge and the fear of the Lord. He will delight in obeying the Lord. He will never judge by appearance, false evidence, or hearsay. He will defend the poor and the exploited. He will rule against the wicked and destroy them with the breath of his mouth. He will be clothed with fairness and truth.

ISAIAH 11:2–5 NLT

The Wise Man's Glory

God's highest priority is that we get to know Him and live a life that reflects His love and justice.

Thus saith the Lord, Let not the wise man glory in his wisdom, neither let the mighty man glory in his might, let not the rich man glory in his riches: But let him that glorieth glory in this, that he understandeth and knoweth me, that I am the Lord which exercise lovingkindness, judgment, and righteousness, in the earth: for in these things I delight, saith the Lord.

JEREMIAH
9:23–24 KJV

Wisdom

Making a Difference

We all want to do something effective in this world while we are here. The key is being faithful to what God lays on our heart.

There is a universal desire among people today: to make a difference. The biggest road-block in finding "where" we can be most effective is not knowing our purpose and our calling. When we make a decision to seek God's wisdom it will mean: getting to know God better so we can apply His wisdom in all our decisions; waiting patiently for God to open and close doors as He engineers our circumstances; and doing what is closest at hand that we know is God's will. For example: God's  concern for the poor is evident in nearly every book of the Bible. Central to following God is seeing that the poor and oppressed around us are treated fairly. When we cultivate a compassionate spirit, we mirror God's love and concern for a needy world.

God has given each of us a purpose for living, and when we are serious about wanting to know it and faithful to obey what He shows us, we can trust Him to guide us into that place of His perfect will.

When did you last pause to recognize God's wisdom in the timing of events in your life? Have you thanked Him?

Wisdom Speaks

Listen as wisdom calls out! Hear as understanding raises her voice! She stands on the hilltop and at the crossroads. At the entrance to the city, at the city gates, she cried aloud, "I call to you, to all of you! I am raising my voice to all people. How naïve you are! Let me give you common sense. O foolish ones, let me give you understanding. Listen to me! For I have excellent things to tell you. Everything I say is right, for I speak the truth and hate every kind of deception. My advice is wholesome and good. There is nothing crooked or twisted in it. My words are plain to anyone with understanding, clear to those who want to learn.

"Choose my instruction rather than silver, and knowledge over pure gold. For wisdom is far more valuable than rubies. Nothing you desire can be compared with it.

"I, Wisdom, live together with good judgment. I know where to discover knowledge and discernment. All who fear the Lord will hate evil. That is why I hate pride, arrogance, corruption, and perverted speech. Good advice and success belong to me. Insight and strength are mine. Because of me, kings reign, and rulers make just laws. Rulers lead with my help, and nobles make righteous judgments.

"I love all who love me. Those who search for me will surely find me. Unending riches, honor, wealth, and justice are mine to distribute. My gifts are better than the purest gold, my wages better than sterling silver! I walk in righteousness, in paths of justice. Those who love me inherit wealth, for I fill their treasuries.

"The Lord formed me from the beginning, before he created anything else. I was appointed in ages past, at the very first, before the earth began. I was born before the oceans were created, before the springs bubbled forth their waters. Before the mountains and the hills were formed, I was born—before he had made the earth and fields and the first handfuls of soil.

"I was there when he established the heavens, when he drew the horizon on the oceans. I was there when he set the clouds above, when he established the deep fountains of the earth. I was there when he set the limits of the seas, so they would not spread beyond their boundaries. And when he marked off the earth's foundations, I was the architect at his side. I was his constant delight, rejoicing always in his presence. And how happy I was with what he created—his wide world and all the human family!

"And so, my children, listen to me, for happy are all who follow my ways. Listen to my counsel and be wise. Don't ignore it.

"Happy are those who listen to me, watching for me daily at my gates, waiting for me outside my home! For whoever finds me finds life and wins approval from the Lord. But those who miss me have injured themselves. All who hate me love death."

PROVERBS 8 NLT

If You Need Wisdom, Ask God

If any of you need wisdom, you should ask God, and it will be given to you. God is generous and won't correct you for asking. But when you ask for something, you must have faith and not doubt. Anyone who doubts is like an ocean wave tossed around in a storm. If you are that kind of person, you can't make up your mind, and you surely can't be trusted. So don't expect the Lord to give you anything at all.

JAMES 1:5–8 THE PROMISE

Wisdom:
The Sought-After Virtue

Having knowledge is not the same as having wisdom. The true test of wisdom is knowing how and when to act, according to God's will.

Rare and scarce,
precious and priceless,
inestimable and invaluable.

These are just a few words which describe that desirable attribute, that much sought after virtue which men call wisdom. English poet Samuel Taylor Coleridge once wrote, "Common sense in an uncommon degree is what the world calls wisdom." Webster puts it this way, "Wisdom is the quality of being wise; it is knowledge with capacity to use it; it is the perception of the best ends and the best means."

Wisdom is that virtue which enables a man to make decisions as God would make them. Putting it another way, a wise man is one who solves his problems in the same manner as God would solve them. . . . One commentator wrote, "Through knowledge man has learned to travel faster than sound but shows his lack of wisdom by going faster in the wrong direction." Charles Haddon Spurgeon had it right when he said, "Wisdom is the right use of knowledge. To know is not to be wise. Many men know a great deal and are all the greater fools for it. There is no fool so great a fool as a knowing fool. But to know how to use knowledge is to have wisdom."

True wisdom is available to man through prayer. One day David found himself involved in a battle with the Philistines in the Valley of Rephaim. God instructed David to encircle the enemy and come in from behind at the point where the mulberry trees were located. He was told that when he heard a stirring in those trees, he was to begin the attack. This he did, carrying out God's counsel to the letter. As a result he won an overwhelming victory (2 Samuel 5:22–25).

HAROLD L. FICKETT, JR., *JAMES*

Wisdom is a tree of life to those who embrace her; happy are those who hold her tightly. PROVERBS 3:18 NLT

True spiritual maturity, the product of time spent in the Word and continuous walking in the Spirit, manifests itself when Christ's will and your will are synonymous.

TIM LaHAYE, *How to Win over Depression*

To Know God—Study Him

I wish you could truly begin the study of God. This must be our delight throughout eternity. It is the happiest and most helpful study that can possibly engage our thoughts. Why cannot we know God without study? Because all knowledge is thus acquired. To learn a thing without study is to forget it. To learn and not use, is also to forget. Life is unhappy to many because they know so little of God. Those who know Him best are most anxious to know more of Him.

DAVID C. COOK, *THE SECRET OF HAPPY HOME-LIFE*

Christianity makes one educated, cultured, and moral, but these things do not make a Christian.

AUTHOR UNKNOWN

From a wise man comes careful and persuasive speech.

PROVERBS 16:23 LB

The Eternal God Is Thy Refuge

H. O. Van Gilder, a past president of Western Baptist College, told this story on several occasions during chapel services in the 1960s. It reminds us that wisdom includes not just knowing, but also trusting and doing.

Recently, we heard of a building project where workmen were working throughout the night. One of the workmen, alone on the edge of a wall several stories high, suddenly lost his balance and fell. Grasping wildly, he was able to grip the edge of the wall with his fingers.

Desperately, he clung to the narrow ledge, hoping soon to be discovered. In the dark shadows below the level of the wall, his shouts and cries for help were to no avail. The noise and chatter of the riveting machines, the puffing of the hoisting engines, and the myriad other sounds in the huge construction project muffled all his calls.

Soon he felt his arms grow numb. Even with intense effort to hold his fingers rigid, they began to relax against the heavy strain. Frantically, he tried to pray, but there was no miracle.

At last, his fingers slipped from the wall. With a last retching sob of terror, he fell—about three inches to a scaffold that had been there in the darkness all the time!

How like a lot of Christians! Thinking their salvation depends on their own endurance, and conscious of their weakness, they are fearful, anxious, and unhappy most of the time. Yet, "underneath are the everlasting arms" (Deuteronomy 33:27 KJV). All the while a faithful, loving, and all-powerful God is waiting to rescue us.

Wisdom

U. S. Presidents on Biblical Wisdom

Throughout the ages, men who've held the United States' highest office have gathered wisdom from the highest authority of all.

George Washington (1732–1799), the first President of the United States, once said, "I now make my earnest prayer that God would be most graciously pleased to dispose us all to do justice, to love mercy, and to demean ourselves with that charity, humility, and pacific temper of mind which were the characteristics of the divine Author of our blessed religion."

President Ulysses S. Grant (1822–1885) said: "Hold fast to the Bible as the sheet anchor of your liberties. Write its precepts in your hearts, and practice them in your lives. To the influence of this Book are we indebted for all the progress made in true civilization, and to this we must look as our guide in the future" (*The Sunday School Times*).

President William McKinley, our 25th President, said: "The more profoundly we study this wonderful book, and the more closely we observe its divine precepts, the better citizens we will become and the higher will be our destiny as a nation."

Theodore Roosevelt (1858–1919), the United States' 26th President, is quoted as saying, "Almost every man who has by his life-work added to the sum of human achievement of which the race is proud, of which our people are proud, almost every such man has based his life-work largely upon the teachings of the Bible."

President Calvin Coolidge (1872–1933), when presented a Bible while in office said, "In this little book will be found the solution to all the problems of the world."

Woodrow Wilson (1856–1924), the 28th President, said: "A man has deprived himself of the best there is in the world who has deprived himself of this [a knowledge of the Bible].... There are a good many problems before the American people today, and before me as President, but I expect to find the solution of those problems just in the proportion that I

284

am faithful in the study of the Word of God."

President Herbert Hoover (1874–1964) said, "There is no other book so varied as the Bible, nor one so full of concentrated wisdom. Whether it be of law, business, morals, or that vision which leads the imagination in the creation of constructive enterprise for the happiness of mankind, he who seeks for guidance in any of these things may look inside its covers and find illumination. The study of this Book in your Bible classes is a post-graduate course in the richest library of human experience. As a nation we are indebted to the Book of books for our national ideas and representative institutions. Their preservation rests in adhering to its principles."

And President Jimmy Carter said, "We believe that the first time we're born, as children, it's human life given to us; and when we accept Jesus as our Savior, it's a new life. That's what 'born again' means."

Acquire Wisdom

Get wisdom, get understanding;
do not forget my words or swerve
    from them.
Do not forsake wisdom, and she
    will protect you;
love her, and she will watch over
    you.
Wisdom is supreme; therefore get
    wisdom.
Though it cost all you have, get
    understanding.

PROVERBS 4:5–7 NIV

Wisdom

Wise Words and Important Truths

It is important that a wise person passes on their wisdom—not only in words, but in deeds.

Because the Teacher was wise, he taught the people everything he knew. He collected proverbs and classified them. Indeed, the Teacher taught the plain truth, and he did so in an interesting way.

A wise teacher's words spur students to action and emphasize important truths. The collected sayings of the wise are like guidance from a shepherd.

But, my child, be warned: There is no end of opinions ready to be expressed. Studying them can go on forever and become very exhausting!

Here is my final conclusion: Fear God and obey his commands, for this is the duty of every person. God will judge us for everything we do, including every secret thing, whether good or bad.

Ecclesiastes 12:9–13 NLT

Growing in wisdom means growing in love, tolerance, grace, and acceptance.

Did I Do It?

Instead of asking yourself whether you believe or not, ask yourself whether you have this day done one thing because He said, *Do it,* or once abstained because He said, *Do not do it!* It is simply absurd to say you believe, or even want to believe, in Him, if you do not do anything He tells you.

GEORGE MACDONALD

Following God's Guidance

Whenever we are uncertain as to our course, we can rely on God, in His wisdom, to shut doors against us—every door but the right one.

God guides His people through His Word, by circumstances, and by the peace in our Spirit. When we are "willing" to follow what we sense that God is telling us to do, we are never left wondering for long as to which way we should go.

When we cooperate with God as He engineers the circumstances of our lives, there is no limit to what He can do. God opens and closes the doors before us at His will. When we don't understand what He is doing, we do well to remember that we are not fulfilled by the plans we create, but rather by following God's plan for us.

And those who are wise—the people of God—shall shine as brightly as the sun's brilliance, and those who turn many to righteousness will glitter like stars forever.

Daniel 12:3 LB

On Prudence in Action

Millions of people through the ages have read the words of Thomas à Kempis and endeavored to put his words into practice in their daily lives.

We should not believe every word and suggestion, but should carefully and unhurriedly consider all things in accordance with the will of God. For such is the weakness of human nature, alas, that evil is often more readily believed and spoken of another than good. But perfect men do not easily believe every tale that is told them, for they know that man's nature is prone to evil, and his words to deception.

It is wise not to be over hasty in action, nor to cling stubbornly to our own opinions. It is wise also not to believe all that we hear, nor to hasten to report to others what we hear or believe. Take counsel of a wise and conscientious man, and seek to be guided by one who is better than yourself, rather than to follow your own opinions. A good life makes a man wise towards God, and gives him experience in many things. The more humble and obedient to God a man is, the more wise and at peace he will be in all that he does.

THOMAS À KEMPIS, *THE IMITATION OF CHRIST*

Wisdom, A New Heart

Jesus challenges the conventional wisdom with a new wisdom of the heart.

The people of Nazareth had seen Jesus grow up. They knew his mother and father, his brothers and sisters. Matthew reports that they were astounded and then offended. How could someone so ordinary be saying what Jesus said? He was judged by his background and by his family. Yet even though the people of Nazareth hated to admit it, Jesus was an amazing teacher.

Jesus was a teacher of widom; his words and his life drew people into the presence of God. In Jesus, people could see a glimpse of God. As a teacher of wisdom, he called and challenged people to center their life on God and to trust that the Maker of the universe was a gracious and compassionate God.

His teaching went against the common wisdom of his day.

The wisdom of Jesus' day—and even today—is concerned with personal identity and security. Wealth and possessions were not only a way to comfort and ease, but they were also thought to be a sign that God looked upon you with favor. Jesus warned of the dangers of riches. "How hard it will be for those who have wealth to enter the kingdom of God!" (Mark 10:23 NRSV). Even though Jesus associated with the rich and had some wealthy supporters, it is clear that Jesus saw money as a distraction from living a godly life, and he saw greed putting blinders on people so they no longer had human compassion. Jesus presented wisdom that was centered on God and service to other people.

In Jesus' day, even religion had become a means to identity and security. People wanted to be a descendant of Abraham

and live according to the rules. The Pharisees thought they were models of religious life because they faithfully adhered to the most rigorous standards of the day. Yet Jesus often criticized the Pharisees because their security was based in their own religious accomplishments. In contrast, Jesus lifted up the example of the tax collector who prayed, "God, be merciful to me, a sinner!" (Luke 18:13 NRSV).

The wisdom that Jesus brought centered on the heart, the deepest center of a person. The religious externals were less important than the motivations. "Blessed are the pure in heart, for they will see God" (Matthew 5:8 NRSV).

The wisdom of Jesus centered on God. A radical trust in God is contrasted with the anxiety of trying to make it on our own. Jesus invited his followers to see that at the heart of everything is a God who loves us.

For his friends in Nazareth, the invitation from Jesus was intriguing and frightening. They could see his wisdom, but they knew the security of possessions and of following the religious leaders. They had their families to think of and their careers to advance. Could they trust God to provide?

We wrestle today with the same invitation. Jesus asks us, "Where is your heart?" Do our activities flow from the center of God's grace and guidance?

A Prayer for Wisdom

Dear Lord, help me to build on a firm foundation by relying on your wisdom, diligently seeking your direction in all I do, learning to walk in your paths of kindness, peace, and justice to others. In Jesus' name, Amen.

*Don't refuse to accept
criticism; get all the help you can.*

PROVERBS 23:12 LB

*Wisdom comes through a constant process of
growth! Don't depend on inspiration or
luck—plan to prevail by good planning and
steady work.*

LIFE APPLICATION BIBLE NOTES (PROVERBS 2:10 LB)

Wisdom

The intelligent man is always open to new ideas. In fact, he looks for them.

PROVERBS 18:15 LB

What Would Jesus Do?

In 1935, the book In His Steps *was the most popular book—with the exception of the Bible—that had ever been written. Over 30,000,000 copies were sold in all corners of the world and in many languages. The theme of the book is as relevant today as ever.*

Henry Maxwell's face was wet with tears. If an audible voice from heaven had sanctioned their pledge to follow the Master's steps, not one person present could have felt more certain of the divine blessing. And so the most serious movement ever started in the First Church of Raymond was begun.

"We all understand," said he, speaking very quietly, "what we have undertaken to do. We pledge ourselves to do everything in our daily lives after asking the question, 'What would Jesus do?' regardless of what may be the result to us. Some time I shall be able to tell you what a marvelous change has come over my life within a week's time. I cannot now. But the experience I have been through since last Sunday has left me so dissatisfied with my previous definition of Christian discipleship that I have been compelled to take this action. I did not dare begin it alone. I know that I am being led by the hand of divine love in all this. The same divine impulse must have led you also.

"Do we understand fully what we have undertaken?"

CHARLES SHELDON, *IN HIS STEPS*

In His Own Words . . . About *In His Steps*

A fundamental part of wisdom is having access to information. Here, Charles Sheldon explains in the foreword how, through a happy "accident," In His Steps became the second most widely distributed book of its time.

The story "In His Steps" was written in 1896, and it was read a chapter at a time to my young people, Sunday evenings in the Central Congregational Church, Topeka, Kansas. While it was being read it was being published in the *Chicago Advance*, a religious weekly, as a serial. The publisher did not know the conditions of the copyright law, and he filed only one copy of the *Advance* each week with the department, instead of two, which the law required. On that account the copyright was defective, and the story was thrown into the "public domain" when the Advance Company put it out in a ten cent paper edition. Owing to the fact that no one had any legal ownership in the book, sixteen different publishers in America and fifty in Europe and Australia put out the book in various editions from an English penny to eight shillings. Mr. Bowden, the London publisher, sold over 3,000,000 copies of the penny edition on the streets of London.

The book has been translated into twenty-one languages, including a Russian publication which has been banned by the Soviet. A Turkish translation in Arabic is permitted circulation by the government and is being read all over Turkey.

The story has been made into the drama form and is being used by groups of young church people and by college students. And while conditions have changed in the years since the story was written, the principle of human conduct remains the same. I do not need to say that I am very thankful that owing to the defective copyright, the book has had a larger reading on account of the great number of publishers. I find readers in every part of the world where I go. And I am informed by the *Publishers' Weekly* that the book has had more circulation than any other book except the Bible. If that is true, no one is more grateful than I am, as it confirms the faith I have always held that no subject is more interesting and vital to the human race than religion.

CHARLES SHELDON

Lord, Let Me See

Some people are unable to see because of damage to or a defect in their eyes. Others, however, choose not to see, succumbing to egotism or self-righteousness, materialism or prejudice, greed or fear, love of power or even self-hate. Whatever the cause, blindness can result.

Jesus stood still and ordered the man to be brought to him; and when he came near, he asked him, "What do you want me to do for you?" He said, "Lord, let me see again." Jesus said to him, "Receive your sight; your faith has saved you." Immediately he regained his sight and followed him, glorifying God; and all the people, when they saw it, praised God.

LUKE 18:40–43 NRSV

Wisdom

I Know Not Why

*Our lives are filled with many
questions that may never be
answered, but that's okay if we let
God lead and direct us. We may not
understand why certain things
happen or why we have to go
through difficult situations. But the
one thing we can know for sure is
that God is always in charge.*

I know not why His hand is laid
    In chastening on my life,
Nor why it is my little world
    Is filled so full of strife.
I know not why, when faith looks
      up
    To seek release from pain,
That o'er my sky fresh clouds
      arise
    To drench my path with rain.
I know not why my prayer so long
    By Him has been denied,
Nor why, when other ships
      sail on,
    Mine should in port abide.
But I do know that God is love,
    That He my burden bears,
So tho' I do not understand,
    One thing I know … He cares!
I know the heights for which I
      yearn
    Are often reached through
      pain.

I know that sheaves must needs be
      threshed
    To yield their golden grain.
I know that though He may
      remove
    The friends on whom I lean,
'Tis that I thus may learn to love
    And trust the One unseen.
And when at last my race is run,
    And Heaven's joys I've known,
I will not care how rough the road
    That lead through Christ, to
      Home.
For whate'er my lot in life may be,
    One thing I know … He
      leadeth me!

AUTHOR UNKNOWN

Putting Words in Your Mouth

One of life's biggest fears is that when we have to face a frightening event that requires an immediate response, we will simply freeze up and not know what to say or do. Wouldn't it be wonderful to know that the wisdom to handle the situation will be there when you need it?

The phrase, "putting words in my mouth," is usually used when someone is complaining. It means someone is misrepresenting what the person really wants to say.

In effect, the idea of putting words in someone else's mouth is accusing someone of being a ventriloquist. You open your mouth, but the words that emerge are not really your own. You can end up mouthing the wording provided by the other party.

All this sounds pretty diabolical. But there is at least one case in which "putting words in your mouth" could be a very positive thing.

Under religious persecution, people are called and asked to defend their beliefs. They can be faced with suffering, imprisonment, or even death if they don't respond as the persecutors want them to. The very way things are handled is a calculated attempt to

unnerve or terrify the person on trial. If the strategy is successful, the defendants may provide crucial information or even recant their beliefs.

Perhaps the biggest difficulty in attempting to survive this kind of trial is that the person is separated from others. As long as there is a support system, most people can withstand a great deal. But if you feel isolated and all alone, it is much harder to take the pressure.

While persecution of other trials may seem to leave you all alone, that is not the case. The Lord has promised, "I will never leave you or forsake you"; his spiritual presence is always present. But he has also made another incredible promise: He will, somehow, put the right words in your mouth, at the right time, in order for you to defend yourself.

Now, that does not mean that close-minded opposition will be satisfied with what is said. But it does mean that God's viewpoint will get presented powerfully enough to impact someone who is present with an open mind.

History is full of examples of those who did not think they could speak up under such difficult circumstances. Then, when the time came, they heard their own voices speaking eloquent words that were at once their own, yet seemed to come from another source, a higher power.

Being placed on the firing line to defend your faith is not something that most people look forward to. Yet, if it were to happen, it is a great comfort to know that the Lord would provide the wisdom needed to respond properly, at just the right time.

A person can accumulate immense knowledge and still lack wisdom. Wisdom requires compassion, justice, humility, and spiritual discernment.

Wisdom

Seek Wisdom Seriously

We all know people who never find wisdom, because they don't seek it seriously. Wisdom comes easily only to those who pay attention to experienced people and to God. If the wisdom you need does not come easily to you, perhaps your attitude is the barrier.

Life Application Bible Notes (Proverbs 14:6 LB)

Hearing the Truth

A lot of poor advice is worth less than a little good advice. It is easy to get opinions from people who will tell us only what they think will please us, but such advice is not helpful. Instead we should look for those who will speak the truth, even when it hurts. Think about the people to whom you go for advice. What do you expect to hear from them?

Life Application Bible Notes (Proverbs 10:20 LB)

Wisdom

The world will judge our doctrines by our deeds.

AUTHOR UNKNOWN

Who among you is wise and understanding? Let him show by his good behavior his deeds in the gentleness of wisdom.

JAMES 3:13 NAS

Live As Those Who Are Wise

So be careful how you live,
not as fools but as those
who are wise.
Make the most of every
opportunity for doing good
in these evil days.
Don't act thoughtlessly, but
try to understand what the
Lord wants you to do.

EPHESIANS 5:15–17 NLT

When God Asks You to be Wise

God chose what is foolish in the world to shame the wise; God chose
what is weak in the world to shame the strong; God chose what is low
and despised in the world, things that are not, to reduce to nothing
things that are, so that no one might boast in the presence of God.
He is the source of our life in Christ Jesus, who became for us wisdom
from God.

1 CORINTHIANS 1:27–30 NRSV

Joy

When we think of joy, we often think of things that are new—a new day, a new baby, a new love, a new beginning, the promise of a new home with God in heaven. Rejoicing in these things originates with having joy in the God who makes all things new. Rather than relying on earthly pleasures to provide happiness, the Scriptures command that we rejoice in God and in each new day He brings. Joy is a celebration of the heart that goes beyond circumstances to the very foundation of joy—the knowledge that we are loved by God.

Shout for Joy!

When we experience true joy, we will naturally express it. As God pours joy into our lives, we can bring it back to Him.

Shout for joy to the Lord, all the earth. Worship the Lord with gladness; come before him with joyful songs. Know that the Lord is God. It is he who made us, and we are his; we are his people, the sheep of his pasture. Enter his gates with thanksgiving and his courts with praise; give thanks to him and praise his name. For the Lord is good and his love endures forever; his faithfulness continues through all generations.

PSALM 100 NIV

Rejoice in the Lord always; again I will say, rejoice!

PHILIPPIANS 4:4 NASB

Though now you do not see Him, yet believing, you rejoice with joy inexpressible and full of glory.

1 PETER 1:8 NKJV

Dance for Joy

Cultures throughout the world have used dance to express joy. Dancing is done at feasts, at weddings, and at almost every other celebration. In fact, God's word commands us to dance as an expression of worship and joy.

For all those who are afraid to dance for joy, here is a challenge. Go home and put on your favorite music that honors God. Listen to the words carefully or put on classical music, which speaks without words. Let the burdens and cares of life float away. Contemplate all God has done for you. Think about the loving family you have. Think of all the times God has saved them from harm when your arms of protection weren't long enough. Remember the times God rescued you from hopelessness and depression. Think of how so many sorrows have passed when it seemed they never could. Concentrate on the love of God—the wonder of His plan for humankind—the fact that the God of the universe wants a love relationship with us—with you. Think about the truth that if you were the only one on earth, Jesus would

have laid down His life for you—you count that much with Him. Think of what your heavenly home will be like. Think of the mansion and streets of gold that await you. Think of dancing on those streets as you go to meet your departed loved ones and see Jesus face to face. Let your feet and your body respond to the joy that is in you. Dare to dance as an expression of joy.

How can dancing be wrong when Scripture says, "You have turned for me my mourning into dancing" (Psalm 30:11 NKJV)? And what about the celebration when the prodigal son came home? Scripture says that the older son "heard music and dancing" as part of the celebration (Luke 15:25). There was the dancing in celebration after the Israelites had crossed the Red Sea: "Then Miriam, the prophetess, Aaron's sister, took a tambourine in her hand, and all the women followed her, with tambourines and dancing" (Exodus 15:20 NIV). And was it wrong when David "danced before the Lord with all his might . . . leaping and whirling before the Lord" (2 Samuel 2:14, 16)? Psalm 149:3 gives this instruction: "Praise Him

with the timbrel and dance . . ."
Ecclesiastes says there is "a time to
mourn, and a time to dance . . ."
(verse 4).

Every place in Scripture that
refers to dancing has to do with
rejoicing. It is one way to
rejoice before God and in
God. Certainly one can
choose a dance that rejoices
in vulgarity or sensuous-
ness or worldliness, but
does that mean we cannot
choose to rejoice in the
Lord through dancing?
Dance before the Lord as
David did. Let Him lead.

There is much to
rejoice about. Let fear
and inhibition depart. Go
ahead—dance for joy.

Weeping may endure for a night,
but joy cometh in the morning.

PSALM 30:5 KJV

Free to Show Joy

It is wonderful to watch an uninhibited person express joy. We long to give our souls permission to rejoice so freely.

My rosy-cheeked boy stood still, watching with wide-eyed fascination the gyrating dance of the Down syndrome girl as she scooped up leaves and showered herself with a twirling rain of autumn jubilation.

With each twist and hop she sang, deep, earthy grunts—a canticle of praise meant only for the One whose breath causes the leaves to tremble from the trees.

Hurry up. Let's go. Seat belts on? I start the car. In the rearview mirror I study her one more time through misty eyes. And then the tears come. Not tears of pity for her. The tears are for me. For I am too busy to dance in the autumn leaves and far too sophisticated to publicly shout praises to my Creator.

I am whole and intelligent and normal, and so I weep because I will never know the severe mercy that frees such a child and bids her come dance in the autumn leaves.

ROBIN JONES GUNN, "AUTUMN DANCE"

When Laughter Fades

Laughter is such a part of joy that when it fades in a loved one, our hearts can feel like they are about to break. The return of laughter brings renewed joy.

One of the worst things about my ten-month-old's sickness, which the doctors called "failure to thrive" and which led to weeks in the hospital, was when she reached a point where she did not laugh. Before she got sick, she loved to repeatedly cover and uncover her eyes and laugh heartily every time I said, "Peek-a-boo." Often I'd tickle her tummy and say, "Coochie, coochie coo," as she laughed gleefully. I tried these when she was in the hospital. It broke my heart that she would not, could not laugh or even smile.

I remember the day I wearily prayed, telling God how much I missed her laughter. Shortly after, I went up to her room, and for the first time in days, she played all the little games, and she laughed and laughed. It was like medicine to my soul. The next day, the laughter disappeared again, but it was enough to help me through the rest of her illness. She is a healthy teen now, and I still love to hear the sound of her laughter.

I wonder, does God love to hear the sound of our laughter? Does it break His heart too when we are no longer able or willing to laugh for joy? Does it lift Him up when we resume our laughter? I believe the answer to these questions is "Yes. Yes. Yes."

Sweet Sorrow

It seems whatever brings us the greatest joy also brings sorrow. Every mother knows that. We would not feel such sorrow if we did not have such great love for our children.

The Sorrow Tugs

There's a lot of joy in the smiling
world,
    there's plenty of morning sun,
And laughter and songs and
    dances, too
    whenever the day's work's
    done;
Full many an hour is a shining
    one, when
    viewed by itself apart,
But the golden threads in the
    warp of life are
    the sorrow tugs at your heart.

Oh, the fun is froth and it blows
    away, and
    many a joy's forgot,
And the pleasures come and the
    pleasures go,

and memory holds them not;
But treasured ever you keep the
    pain that causes
    your tears to start,
For the sweetest hours are the
    ones that bring
    the sorrow tugs at your heart.

The lump in your throat and the
    little sigh when
    your baby trudged away
The very first time to the big red
    school—how
    long will the memory stay?
The fever days and the long black
    night you
    watched as she troubled, slept,
And the joy you felt when she
    smiled once
    more—how long will that all
    be kept?

The glad hours live in a feeble
    way, but the sad
    ones never die.
His first long trousers caused a
    pang and you
    saw them with a sigh.

And the big still house when the
  boy and girl,
    unto youth and beauty grown,
To college went; will you e'er
    forget that first
    grim hour alone?

It seems as you look back over
    things, that all
    that you treasure dear

Is somehow blent in a wondrous
    way with a
    heart pang and a tear.
Though many a day is a joyous
    one when
    viewed by itself apart,
The golden threads in the warp of
    life are the
    sorrow tugs at your heart.

EDGAR A. GUEST, *A Heap o' Livin'*

Trust Means Joy

We can maintain our joy when we remember how faithful and unchanging God is. Focusing on Him brings renewed joy.

The root of faith produces the flower of heart-joy. We may not at the first rejoice, but it comes in due time. We trust the Lord when we are sad, and in due season He so answers our confidence that our faith turns to fruition and we rejoice in the Lord. Doubt breeds distress, but trust means joy in the long run....

Let us meditate upon the Lord's holy name, that we may trust Him the better and rejoice the more readily. He is in character holy, just, true, gracious, faithful and unchanging. Is not such a God to be trusted? He is allwise, almighty, and everywhere present; can we not cheerfully rely on Him? ... They that know thy name will trust thee; and they that trust thee will rejoice in thee, O Lord.

CHARLES SPURGEON, *Faith's Checkbook*

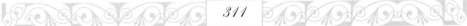

The Lost Is Found

There is great joy when lost things are found—lost lambs, lost coins, but especially lost people. Sometimes we lose our joy, like the older brother in the story of the prodigal son. The good news is that we can turn to God and find it again.

"Suppose one of you had a hundred sheep and lost one. Wouldn't you leave the ninety-nine in the wilderness and go after the lost one until you found it? When found, you can be sure you would put it across your shoulders, rejoicing, and when you got home call in your friends and neighbors, saying, 'Celebrate with me! I've found my lost sheep!' Count on it—there's more joy in heaven over one sinner's rescued life than over ninety-nine good people in no need of rescue.

"Or imagine a woman who has ten coins and loses one. Won't she light a lamp and scour the house, looking in every nook and cranny until she finds it?

And when she finds it you can be sure she'll call her friends and neighbors: 'Celebrate with me! I found my lost coin!' Count on it—that's the kind of party God's angels throw every time one lost soul turns to God."

Then he said, "There was once a man who had two sons. The younger said to his father, 'Father, I want right now what's coming to me.'

"So the father divided the property between them. It wasn't long before the younger son packed his bags and left for a distant country. There, undisciplined and dissipated, he wasted everything he had. After he had gone through all his money, there was a bad famine all through that country and he began to hurt. He signed on with a citizen there who assigned him to his fields to slop the pigs. He was so hungry he would have eaten the corncobs in the pig slop, but no one would give him any.

"That brought him to his senses. He said, 'All those farmhands working for my father sit down to three meals a day, and here I am starving to death. I'm going back to my father. I'll say to him, "Father, I've sinned against God, I've sinned before you; I don't deserve to be called your son. Take me on as a hired hand."' He got right up and went home to his father.

"When he was still a long way off, his father saw him. His heart pounding, he ran out, embraced him, and kissed him. The son started his speech: 'Father, I've sinned against God, I've sinned before you; I don't deserve to be called your son ever again.'

"But the father wasn't listening. He was calling to the servants, 'Quick. Bring a clean set of clothes and dress him. Put the family ring on his finger and sandals on his feet. Then get a grain-fed heifer and roast it. We're going to feast! We're going to have a wonderful time! My son is here—given up for dead and now alive! Given up

for lost and now found!' And they began to have a wonderful time.

"All this time the older son was out in the field. When the day's work was done he came in. As he approached the house, he heard the music and dancing. Calling over one of the houseboys, he asked what was going on. He told him, 'Your brother came home. Your father has ordered a feast—barbecued beef!—because he has him home safe and sound!'

"The older brother stalked off in an angry sulk and refused to join in. His father came out and tried to talk to him, but he wouldn't listen. The son said, 'Look how many years I've stayed here serving you, never giving you one moment of grief, but have you ever thrown a party for me and my friends? Then this son of yours who has thrown away your money on whores shows up and you go all out with a feast!'

"His father said, 'Son, you don't understand. You're with me all the time, and everything that is mine is yours—but this is a wonderful time, and we had to celebrate. This brother of yours was dead, and he's alive! He was lost, and he's found!'"

LUKE 15:3–32 THE MESSAGE

Joy is the inner celebration that nothing on the outside can change the fact that God loves me.

Joy Goes Beyond Happiness

How wonderful that God wants us to go beyond the pursuit of happiness to experience joy. We can be joyful even when we're unhappy.

All sorts of things can undermine happiness—time, change, and tragedy above all. There isn't anything intrinsically wrong with happiness, but trying to build on just the right set of circumstances is too insecure a base...

But the answer is not to reject happiness, it is to go beyond it, to joy.... Joy is different from happiness because of the cause of the ultimacy of its fulfillment and because it is a profound reality regardless of our circumstances. Rooted in God, empowered by the energies of the resurrection, joy does not depend on getting the right income, the perfect spouse, the right mix of things. Joy goes so far beyond happiness that it is present even in the midst of deep unhappiness.

REBECCA MANLEY PIPPERT, *HOPE HAS ITS REASONS*

Joy from the Vine

Many try to find joy in the fruit of the vine—wine. But true and lasting joy comes from the true vine—Jesus.

Remember, in the first place, that the Vine was the Eastern symbol of Joy. It was its fruit that made glad the heart of man. Yet, however innocent that gladness—for the expressed juice of the grape was the common drink at every peasant's board—the gladness was only a gross and passing thing. This was not true happiness, and the vine of the Palestine vineyards was not the true vine. *"Christ* was the *true* Vine." Here, then, is the ultimate source of Joy. Through whatever media it reaches us, all true Joy and Gladness find their source in Christ.

HENRY DRUMMOND, *THE GREATEST THING IN THE WORLD*

Happiness and Joy

We all want to be happy, but joy goes much deeper. Joy is not based on circumstances or feelings, which change like the weather. True joy comes from a celebration of the heart over the things that do not change—things that come from the Lord.

The desire of happiness, beyond all doubt, is a natural desire. It is the law of life itself that every being seeks and strives toward the perfection of its kind, the realization of its own specific idea in form and function, and a true harmony with its environment. Every drop of sap in the tree flows toward foliage and fruit. Every drop of blood in the bird beats toward flight and song. In a conscious being this move-ment toward perfection must take a conscious form. This conscious form is happiness,—the satisfaction of the vital impulse,—the rhythm of the inward life,—the melody of a heart that has found its keynote. To say that all men long for this is simply to confess that all men are human, and that their thoughts and feelings are an essential part of their life. Virtue means a completed manhood. The joyful welfare of the soul belongs to the fulness of that ideal. Holiness is wholeness. In striving to realize the true aim of our being, we find the wish for happiness implanted in the very heart of our effort. . . .

Men are not wrong in wishing for happiness, but wrong in their way of seeking it. *Earthly happiness*,—pleasure that belongs to the senses and perishes with them,—

earthly happiness is a dream and a delusion. But *happiness on earth*,—spiritual joy and peace, blossoming here, fruiting here-after,—immortal happiness, is the keynote of life in Christ.

And if we come to Him, He tells us four great secrets in regard to it.

i. It is inward, and not outward; and so it does not depend on what we have, but on what we are.

ii. It cannot be found by direct seeking, but by setting our faces toward the things from which it flows; and so we must climb the mount if we would see the vision, we must tune the instrument if we would hear the music.

iii. It is not solitary, but social; and so we can never have it without sharing it with others.

iv. It is the result of God's will for us, and not of our will for ourselves; and so we can only find it by giving our lives up, in submission and obedience, to the control of God....

This is the divine doctrine of happiness as Christ taught by His life and with His lips. If we want to put it into a single phrase, I know not where we shall find a more perfect utterance than in the words which have been taught us in childhood, —words so strong, so noble, so cheerful, that they summon the heart of manhood like marching music: "Man's chief end is to glorify God and enjoy Him forever."

HENRY VAN DYKE, *COUNSELS BY THE WAY*

Open Up to Joy

We miss so much joy just because we don't open ourselves up to all there is to enjoy. We can choose to embrace all the joy that today has to bring.

There are joys which long to be ours. God sends ten thousand truths, which come about us like birds seeking inlet; but we are shut up to them, and so they bring us nothing, but sit and sing a while upon the roof and then fly away.

HENRY WARD BEECHER, *LIFE THOUGHTS*

Prayer for Joy

Pressures in our lives can crowd out joy. Let's remember to pray and ask God to help us discover renewed joy.

Lord God, I am not always thankful enough that I am a Christian. When I stop to think of all the blessings that come to me because I believe in You, I can only say that Your love for me is the greatest thing that has ever happened to me. Make me properly thankful for Your love, and let me never fail to be happy about it.

Help me to find real joy in worshiping You in church. Help me to sing the truths of the wonderful hymns with my heart as well as my lips. What I hear with my ear, send down deep into my heart. Let the joy of belonging to Jesus show itself in my words and actions, and make me a blessing to my family and friends.

Help me to share my joy of salvation with others. So many people are discouraged and disappointed over both little and large matters. Help me to say and do the right thing at the right time, that my friends may also find their happiness in Jesus on earth and joy with Him in heaven. Bless me in this for Jesus' sake. Amen.

Teenagers Pray

The Joy of Discovery

When we discover the treasures of life, joy follows. Imagine the joy at discovering how to use language—how to communicate. Helen Keller shares the joy of this exciting discovery in her life.

We walked down the path to the well-house, attracted by the fragrance of the honeysuckle with which it was covered. Someone was drawing water and my teacher placed my hand under the spout. As the cool stream gushed over one hand she spelled into the other the word *water,* first slowly, then rapidly. I stood still, my whole attention fixed upon the motions of her fingers. Suddenly I felt a misty consciousness as of something forgotten—a thrill of returning thought; and somehow the mystery of language was revealed to me. I knew then that "w-a-t-e-r" meant the wonderful cool something that was flowing over my hand. That living word awakened my soul, gave it light, hope, joy, set it free! There were barriers still, it is true, but barriers that could in time be swept away.

I left the house eager to learn. Everything had a name, and each name gave birth to a new thought.

As we returned to the house every object which I touched seemed to quiver with life. That was because I saw everything with the strange, new sight that had come to me. On entering the door I remembered the doll I had broken. I felt my way to the hearth and picked up the pieces. I had tried vainly to put them together. Then my eyes filled with tears; for I realized what I had done, and for the first time I felt repentance and sorrow.

I learned a great many new words that day. I do not remember what they all were; but I do know that *mother, father, sister, teacher* were among them—words that were to make the world blossom for me, "like Aaron's rod with flowers." It would have been difficult to find a happier child than I was as I lay in my crib at the close of that eventful day and lived over the joys it had brought me, and for the first time I longed for a new day to come.

HELEN KELLER, *THE STORY OF MY LIFE*

The Flow of Joy

Sometimes I demand,
"God give me joy!"
and nothing happens.
Yet joy flows naturally,
lavishly,
when I seek to
know Him,
love Him, and
serve Him.

Your joy comes from what you give, not from what you accumulate.

FRANK C. LAUBACH, *PRAYER: THE MIGHTIEST FORCE IN THE WORLD*

*In Your presence is fullness of joy;
At Your right hand are pleasures forevermore.*

PSALM 16:11 NKJV